CONTENTS

SAVANNAH AREA
Tourism Leadership Council

Greetings!

On behalf of the local tourism and hospitality industry, welcome to Savannah and Tybee Island, GA! With our unique blend of history, renowned architecture, excellent shopping, world famous dining, magnificent waterways, relaxing beaches and lovely green spaces, your visit is sure to be memorable.

The Savannah Area Tourism Leadership Council (TLC) is excited to share our print journey of the most beautiful city in North America with each of you. It is our sincere hope that you learn something inside the pages of this book that you didn't already know about our area and will be inspired to immerse yourself in the sights, sounds and sensations of our charming city. Experience your own journey through Savannah!

The TLC represents one of the most vibrant and important industries in Savannah. With a diverse workforce nearly 20,000 strong, we graciously welcome more than 6 million visitors to our area each year. Our paramount goal is that each of you have a pleasant and comfortable stay. We lead the charge in education and advocacy efforts for Savannah's tourism community in an effort to ensure that our industry remains healthy. We continually offer local tourism and hospitality businesses opportunities to improve themselves so that they can provide you—our visitors—with the very best experience possible.

Enjoy YOUR Southern journey and we look forward to welcoming you back again soon!

Warm Regards,

Marti Barrow

Marti Barrow
Executive Director
Savannah Area Tourism Leadership Council

© Bryan Stovall

© Bryan Stovall

Welcome to Savannah

"Top Ten U.S. Cities" - *Condé Nast Traveler Magazine*, November 2010

"Most Haunted City in America" - *CNBC.com*, October 2010

"Top 10 Spookiest Cities in the World" - *MSN.com*, October 2010

"Savannah's River Street: America's Coolest River Walks" - *Travel + Leisure Magazine*, September 2010

"USA's Best Ice Cream Parlors: Leopold's Ice Cream" - *USA Today*, August 2010

"Gold Service Award-2010" - *Meetings & Conventions Magazine*, August 2010

"Top 25 Arts Destinations" - *American Style Magazine*, June 2010

"Travelers Choice Destination" - *TripAdvisor.com*, May, 2010

"Top 10 Romance Destinations in the U.S." - *TripAdvisor.com*, May, 2010

"Top 10 Culture and Sightseeing Destinations in the U.S." - *TripAdvisor.com*, April, 2010

"Most Romantic Getaways" - *US Airways Magazine*, February, 2010

"Top Romantic Southern Escapes" - *Southern Living Magazine*, January, 2010

PUBLISHER
Tourism Leadership Council
Marti Barrow, *Executive Director*
Jaclyn Schott, *Marketing and Member Services Manager*
Leigh Anne DiVito, *Administrative Assistant*

MANAGING EDITOR
Jessica Leigh Lebos

CONTRIBUTING WRITERS
Laura Clark
Gloria Greenbaum
Allison Hersh
Buffy Nelson
Carrie J. Rodgers
Patrick Rodgers
Tim Rutherford

CREATIVE DESIGNER
Abigail Carter Gravino

PHOTOGRAPHER
Bryan Stovall

CONTRIBUTING PHOTOGRAPHERS
Angela Hopper
Erin Adams
Kevin Nightingale

Published by the Savannah Area Tourism Leadership Council
www.tourismleadershipcouncil.com
P.O.Box 10010, Savannah, Georgia 31412

ISBN 978-0-615-41733-2
Printed in Canada

4

© Bryan Stovall

Spend your vacation with the *Sand Gnats*

Savannah

GRAYSON STADIUM

Historic Grayson Stadium
Where families come to play.
For tickets, call 912-351-9150 or visit **SANDGNATS**

8

Grouper Florentine, The Shrimp Factory

dine|*savannah*

for the discerning palate | what the heck are grits | from the sea to your plate | guide to greens | dishing with paula deen | it's all about the barbecue

Any good traveler knows that no journey should be embarked upon without an informed idea of where and what to eat. After all, you've got to keep up your strength to enjoy the rest of your trip to its fullest, and there's not a person alive who can appreciate even the most fascinating attractions on an empty stomach. Dining out in Savannah is more than simple sustenance—it's an experience that nourishes the body and feeds the soul. Whether you're sampling New American cuisine with wine pairings recommended by the house sommelier or feasting on down-home cooking at a family-style buffet with a half a dozen strangers, you're bound to come away with a pleased palate and new friends. This is an epicurean hub where global influences meet the world's best pit barbecue, and the city's hundreds of restaurants encompass it all to offer unique menus and exquisite hospitality you won't find anywhere but Savannah. We hope you've brought your appetite—and your sense of adventure.

For the
Discerning Palate

SAVANNAH'S #1 FOODIE TAKES A TOUR OF SAVANNAH'S HAUTE CUISINE

By Tim Rutherford

© Ruth's Chris Steak House

Barely more than a decade ago, visitors to Savannah could count its leading-edge, fine dining restaurants on one hand. An infusion of visitors in the mid-to-late 1990s, fueled by the 1996 Olympic sailing venue and John Berendt's best-selling *Midnight in the Garden of Good and Evil*, brought higher expectations, a taste for international cuisine and a hunger that couldn't be ignored. Today, it's excellent to be able to report that there are more choices than you've got fingers and toes.

In the heart of downtown, Chef Christopher Nason brought a decidedly metropolitan flair to the historic Congress Street building that is home to his **Sapphire Grill**. Even before there was a local supply chain to support his menu, Nason wowed locals and visitors with dishes featuring seasonally fresh, one-of-a-kind ingredients flown from all over North America to Savannah. Exotic mushrooms, heirloom tomatoes and other never-before-seen-in-Savannah produce graced his recipes, and Nason built a following that included customers who came by corporate jet for a taste of his menu.

Nason continues to set the standard for culinary integrity. Better local suppliers have reduced his carbon footprint, and sustainability is the new watchword. Still, changing times have not quashed Nason's menu. More than a decade of maturity has mellowed the passionate chef and inched him toward the top of his game. Today, the same philosophies—fresh, unique and exquisite—are still paramount to his mission as he carefully sauces flavorful seafood, coaxes varied nuances from a collection of baby beets or prepares a steak reminiscent of old-school steak houses.

There are the other pioneers who have persevered: **Elizabeth on 37th** founder and Chef Elizabeth Terry won a James Beard Award in 1997, thanks to her innovative new expressions of Southern cuisine and a penchant for local ingredients. Before the term "farm-to-table" was coined, the dishes prepared in this stately Southern mansion were already festooned with herbs and greens fresh from the restaurant's garden. Today, Terry's successor, Chef Kelley Yambor, continues the tradition by utilizing fresh-caught fish, free-range pork and poultry. And yes, the herbs and greens still come fresh from the restaurant garden.

Long before tourism became one of the city's leading industries, locals relied on **The Olde Pink House** for special events, holidays and a place to impress potential clients. The core of the restaurant's menu is built around interpretations or straight-up recreations of traditional Southern cuisine like fresh-caught grouper, collard greens and shrimp and grits. When the restaurant introduced crispy scored flounder topped with a sweet and spicy apricot shallot sauce, the dish quickly became legendary. Here, blackened oysters on the half shell or fried green tomatoes are perfect starters. It's one of the city's most romantic restaurants, with its cozy dining rooms and 19th-century architecture. A recent addition created a large, multi-use space that's perfect for wedding parties and large dinner parties.

For twinkling, candlelit atmosphere amid a historic backdrop, there is no better destination than **Vic's on the River**. General Sherman's troops based there during the Civil War occupation of Savannah and left behind a hand-drawn map that is still visible in the restaurant's main dining room. Narrow windows open onto a commanding view of the riverfront, and an inviting bar is the perfect watering hole for before- or after-dinner drinks. The menu offers Chef Dusty Groves'

© Bryan Stovall

Opposite: Savor a succulent filet from **Ruth's Chris Steak House**, accompanied with the perfect glass of Pinot Noir. *(see ad - page 14) Above:* **The Olde Pink House** is one of Savannah's most romantic dining establishments, with glorious 19th-century decor, plenty of intimate spaces and two different bars to relax in after dinner.

new perspectives on Savannah's indigenous ingredients: pork, duck and, of course, fresh fish and shrimp. East meets West with the pulled pork eggroll with BBQ sauce, hot mustard and peach chutney. Favorite entrées include sweet Wild Georgia Shrimp with cheddar cheese stone ground grits or the tender, juicy cider braised pork shank with maple syrup and smoked bacon whipped sweet potatoes.

With one hand still touching its foundation among New Orleans' finest restaurants and the other on the pulse of 21st-century diners, **Ruth's Chris Steak House** offers traditional, sizzling steaks prepared in its unique, 1,800-degree double broiler and branches out with contemporary dinner specials and purposefully modern flavors. Leading the way among Savannah fine dining establishments, Ruth's Chris features an aggressive schedule of fine wine dinners and tastings with guest wine makers and industry experts—ask your concierge for details. The comfy and cool lounge features local vocalists Thursday, Friday and Saturday nights—a harmonious accompaniment to a perfectly prepared steak or lobster tail with creamed spinach and garlic mashed potatoes. When banana cream pie is on the menu, don't miss this decadence big enough to share!

In search of an intimate setting and world-class cuisine? Go no further than **45 Bistro** in the historic Marshall House Inn. Executive Chef Brian Palefsky has a following among Savannah foodies. His attention to detail and unpretentious dishes exude elegance, a perfect marriage of flavors and accessibility. The menu is an interesting blend of traditional American cuisine and Pan-Asian dishes. The beef carpaccio is sublime, as is Palefsky's tuna version of the same. Choosing an entrée here is like touring the world food scene: Veal Osso Bucco has roots in Milan, England is represented with fish and chips, and there is no more Georgia-influenced dish than the double cut pork chop marinated in Coca-Cola and bourbon, served with collard greens, sweet corn pudding and a drizzle of cherry bourbon reduction. His bento box of sushi and tempura veggies is as at home on the menu as his classic, Savannah-style crab cake. You'll also find a generous, perfectly-seared rack of lamb on the menu.

Some fine dining spots take a unique spin. The setting may be casual at **B. Matthew's Eatery**, but the food, particularly Chef Jeffrey Crumpton's dinner menu, pops with some of the finest flavors and eye-catching presentation the city has to offer. Pecan Crusted Chicken nestles beautifully atop a bed of Mushroom Ravioli, and Smoked Beef over Penne brings mom's stroganoff into the future. This is one of the city's few breakfast-lunch-dinner options. In fact, In July 2010, *Food Network* magazine picked B. Matthews as Georgia's best breakfast!

With barely three dozen seats, **Noble Fare** is built around very personalized, intimate dining. Chef Patrick McNamara masterfully coaxes sauces, reductions and flavored oils into finishing touches that make his plates as beautiful to behold as they are to eat. His wife, Jenny, reigns over a boutique-driven wine list and just may be Savannah's best mixologist.

Alligator Soul's cozy, basement-level dining room is a perfect hideaway to enjoy a meal defined by Chef Chris Dinello's passion for bold flavors and owner Maureen Craig's insistence on exemplary service. Dinello may be the master of big—in flavor, portion and concept—but Maureen, a vegetarian, also insists that Dinello cater to diners who prefer meatless entrées. He absolutely rises to the occasion, sometimes luring a meat eater down the vegetarian path with taste-tempting dishes.

For upscale cuisine with a casual ambience, **Belford's Seafood and Steaks** in City Market holds the corner on casual fine dining. For traditional Southern fare, look no further than the Shrimp, Greens & Grits, but this is also the place to indulge your carnivorous habits with a Kobe beef burger. Vegetarians can sate their appetites with a hearty grilled eggplant dish served over fresh spinach with Portobello mushrooms, roasted red peppers, gorgonzola cheese and a balsamic glaze.

Small plates more your style? **Jazz'd Tapas Bar** has a menu that's sure to please—as well as an extensive martini bar menu and live music five nights a week.

Can't decide? Adventurous (or indecisive) folks can put together your own progressive dining experience—a course at each of your favorites. Many of these restaurants are within an easy walk of one another—or you can catch a quick ride on a pedicab or the city's free **dot** shuttle. Still, with so many Savannah *haute cuisine* experiences to choose from now, you just might have to make another trip! ❁

Above left: **Belford's Seafood and Steaks** in City Market brings a Southern staple to artistic heights with its Shrimp, Greens and Grits plate. *(see ad - page 21) Above right:* Experience a tasty, original take on breakfast, lunch and dinner at **B. Matthew's Eatery** on Bay Street. *(see ad - page 20)*

SIZZLING HOSPITALITY AT ITS FINEST.

At Ruth's Chris, you'll enjoy the ultimate steak experience, where we hand-select our steaks from the top 2% of the nation's beef and serve them to you on sizzling 500° plates to ensure that every bite is hot, juicy and delicious. Located in the heart of Savannah's beautiful historic district, we feature live music and local art so you'll have more than an amazing meal, you'll have an amazing evening.

HISTORIC DOWNTOWN SAVANNAH
912.721.4800 | 111 W. BAY STREET

what the heck are grits?

The creamy concoction known as grits starts with coarsely ground corn kernels that have been cleaned of their hull and germ—also known as "hominy"—then simmered with water or milk until thick.

The Olde Pink House

Vic's on the River

Native Americans once cultivated maize (a form of our modern corn) in these parts, long before European colonists docked on the shores. Legend has it that they offered the settlers grits as a welcome gift.

Grits can be served for breakfast with a pat of butter and a little sugar or they round out hearty lunch and dinner entrees formed into cakes—but they're rarely on a plate alone. We Southerners prefer them next to a heaping serving of scrambled eggs, smothered with sharp cheddar cheese and bacon crumbles. And nothing pleases our palates more than one of "be all and end all" dishes in the Southern culinary repertoire: Wild Georgia Shrimp and grits smothered with gravy.

It's simple enough to re-create your Southern grits experience at home, just make sure you start with the old-fashioned, stone-ground kind—quick grits just aren't the same. —JLL

From the Sea to your Plate

A Guide to Savannah's Seafood

By Buffy Nelson

While consumers all over the country are being encouraged to buy local and support local farmers, Savannahians are proud of the fact that we have been doing this for years—generations is more like it.

As a coastal town, we are fortunate enough to have fresh seafood right off our back porch: We're surrounded by marsh that leads out to the Atlantic Ocean, affording us access to freshwater and saltwater fish all year round—not to mention all the shrimp, oysters, crabs … you get where I'm going with this, right? We've got loads of fresh seafood here, and you're invited to follow as we take a trip to sample Savannah's bounty of seafood and the dishes made from it. We'll even tell you where you can find them—it'd be our pleasure.

Caught Fresh
Now, a little education about the term "local" seafood. The term "local" around here is defined as any seafood caught and brought in on boats that leave and arrive at docks located in Savannah, near its surrounding islands or on the Savannah River. If you've ordered the local catch at a restaurant here, chances are it was swimming in the ocean that morning.

Naturally, Savannah's seafood industry begins with fish. Two of the most popular regional fishes are grouper and flounder, both in abundance in our waters. Both are flaky white fish that are mild in flavor, and the possibilities are endless when a chef has either of them in the kitchen. Other finned creatures you may have the option of ordering are cobia, red snapper, mahi-mahi (also known as dolphinfish) and trigger, all caught at various times of the year right off our coast.

Trey Mathews, the fourth-generation owner of **Mathews Seafood**, knows all about fishing in these waters. For over a hundred years, his family has owned and operated this wholesale and retail seafood distribution business. Mathews buys directly from local fishermen and reports that he supplies roughly 85% of the seafood served in local restaurants. "There is a real family feel to this business for us," says Mathews. "We know where our seafood was caught and who caught it."

The next stop on our journey has to be shrimp. Shrimping is a longstanding industry here in the south, going back several generations. Shrimp is the most popular seafood in the United States, according to **Wild Georgia Shrimp Association**, and between 4.5 and 9 million pounds of white, pink and brown shrimp are harvested off the coast of Georgia each year. (Mathews Seafood alone sells between 2,000 and 3,000 pounds of Wild Georgia shrimp a week.) A fleet of about 500 boats uses trawl nets to harvest shrimp from the sea floor, traveling at speed of two-and-a-half knots (just under three miles per hour.) In the past, concerns developed about the declining sea turtle population, but in recent years, new nets have been developed to help turtles and other larger animals escape while keeping the shrimp.

Inside the Shell
Well, shucks—it's time to talk oysters. Eaten by humans for thousands of years (as evidenced by the ubiquitous piles of consumed shells found at ancient Native American archaeological sites around the world), these tasty bivalve mollusks tend to congregate in intertidal zones like the brackish waters over the Talmadge Bridge in South Carolina. Oyster beds occur naturally and can also be cultivated in "farms" for consistent harvesting. Bagged in burlap and tagged and dated for freshness, the oysters are alive—with their shells snapped shut—until they're ready to be prepared. You can eat 'em raw (by prying apart the shell with a special knife) or eat 'em cooked (they open easier when steamed), but don't ever eat one that's already split its seal—that's asking for real trouble. Oysters that don't open when cooked were dead upon arrival and shouldn't be eaten.

© ROXY and the Roxify Studio

© Angela Hopper Photography

Opposite: Flavors abound in crab cakes served over Savannah red rice and sautéed asparagus from **Belford's Seafood and Steaks**. *(see ad - page 21) Above top:* The grouper over spinach and vermicelli from **River House Seafood** was caught that morning. *(see ad - page 4) Above bottom:* This local blue crab will keep its vibrant color until it finds its way into the cooking pot.

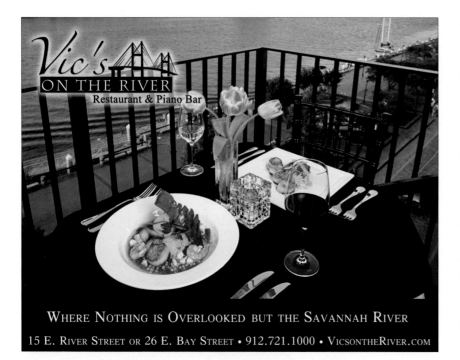

© Angela Hopper Photography

Above: Why choose between clams, crab, oysters and crawfish when you can have them all on one plate at **Fiddlers Crab House**? *(see ad - page 5) Opposite:* There's no silverware necessary with a plate of Lowcountry Boil (which includes shrimp, sausage, corn and potatoes), served up seven days a week at **The Crab Shack** on Tybee Island.

Another local shellfish catch is blue crab, known for its pretty blue exoskeleton and its tasty meat. Commercial crabbers set out pots along the estuaries and rivers and wait for the crabs to crawl in, then they pull up the pots with their catch. Blue crabs turn red when cooked and are the basis for lump meat crab cakes and She-crab soup. At certain times of year before juvenile crabs molt into their hard shells, you can experience the delicacy known as "soft-shell crab."

Place Your Order

Now that our local fishermen, shrimpers and crabbers have caught and sold their wares, it's high time we sat down to eat. With as many varieties of local seafood as we have around here, there's even more ways to cook them—our advice is to continue to let the professionals do what they do best.

Any seafood restaurant worth its name has at least one daily "fresh catch" on the menu—and hopefully more. On historic River Street, **Fiddler's Crab House** (locals just call it Fiddler's) lists its fresh catches outside on a blackboard; the choices will change every day and can come prepared fried, broiled or blackened, depending on your tastes. You can also leave it up to the chef to create something amazing with two or more seafood elements, like flounder stuffed with crab. A chef's special dish that incorporates a fresh catch is a sure bet for a seafood lover with an adventurous palate!

A signature Savannah dish is Crispy Scored Flounder. Several restaurants, including **Garibaldi's** near **City Market**, offer it as a house specialty, and it is indeed quite special! Prepared by "scoring" the skin—shallowly crisscrossing the body with a sharp knife—and fried whole, the dish is presented as the entire fish minus the head, with diamond shaped bites of moist, tasty fish. The presentation is stunning and while it may be a little more work than you're used to putting into eating a piece of fish, it's worth every bite.

If you've spent five minutes in Savannah, you probably already know that shrimp and grits is a staple for breakfast, lunch and dinner. Many establishments offer their unique versions of this classic dish, and there's no such thing as a bad example. That said, **River House Seafood** on the west end of River Street serves up a Low Country Shrimp & Grits that may leave you with permanent cravings! Succulent shrimp that's peppered and grilled served with tasso gravy and stone-ground grits—it's so rich and creamy, the restaurant offers a single portion as an appetizer, or a double portion as an entrée.

Of course, there's more than one way to peel a shrimp, and any restaurant named **The Shrimp Factory** on River Street knows a thing or two about that. Aside from one or two meaty options, this is a shrimp lover's paradise—we recommend the Stuffed Shrimp Savannah. A lunch favorite is the Shrimp Salad Sandwich paired with a crisp Caesar salad prepared tableside. And there's no better way to pass an afternoon than relaxing while slowly peeling your way through a pound of boiled shrimp and dipping them in melted butter or cocktail sauce.

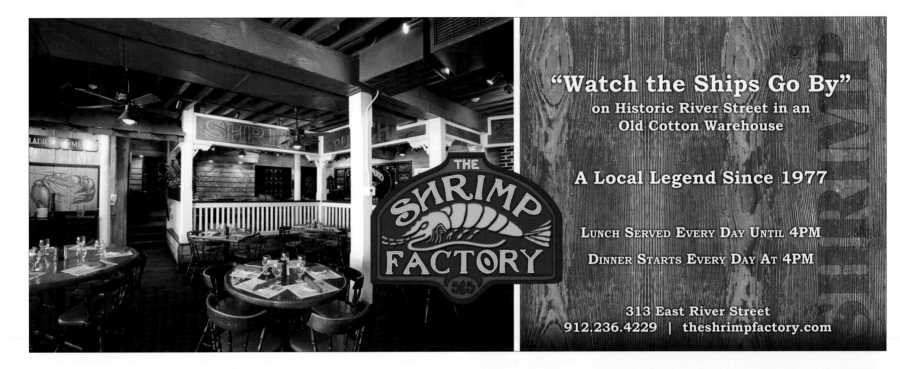
About ten minutes from the historic district towards the ocean, **Uncle Bubba's Oyster House** knows how to keep it simple and delicious. Sold by the dozen (you may end up with several), "Chargrilled Oysters" are nothing but plump, succulent oysters shucked and placed over an open flame to cook in their half shell. Topped with melted butter and Parmesan cheese, they're served with piping hot bread sticks, perfect for sopping up the juices left behind. The oyster "pit" where all the action takes place is located center stage of the main dining area for everyone to see. Only Bubba—the brother of Paula Deen—offers oysters prepared like this, and judging from the packed parking lot, no one can ever get enough.

Of course it's divine to dine on seafood with a view of the water. **The Dolphin Reef Oceanfront Restaurant** on Tybee Island offers an all-you-can-eat seafood buffet with a Caribbean flair. And don't bother changing your shirt for dinner at **The Crab Shack**, a creekside institution that has eschewed silverware, pretensions and even shoes for over 20 years.

Appreciate the Bounty

Seafood is a way of life in Savannah for those who make their living procuring it, for those who prepare it and for those of us lucky enough to sit down to a plate of it. There's a connection between the waters right outside and the food on our plates, and we hope you'll enjoy it all. ❀

© Angela Hopper Photography

© Angela Hopper Photography

GUIDE TO
GREENS

The delicacy known as the Southern "mess o' greens" originated with the African slaves who picked wild plants and flavored them with scraps from the masters' kitchen. They soon learned to cultivate their favorite kinds and have left a delectable legacy on Southern cuisine.

Dark, leafy and full of nutrition, collards are a relative of cabbage and the most popular type of greens found at the Southern table. Mustard greens—the leaves of the plant that yield the spicy yellow flower that becomes the favorite condiment on hot dogs—are also prevalent, as are kale and turnip greens.

Slightly bitter when raw, greens usually get a healthy dose of flavoring in the pot, so just because it's a plate of veggies doesn't necessarily mean it's appropriate for vegetarians: Most Southerners steep their greens with a smoked turkey leg or ham hock. Cooked slowly, they yield a tasty juice called "pot likker" savored by true connoisseurs of Southern cuisine.

Southern greens also have more purpose than satisfying the belly: There's a traditional dish called "Hoppin' John" made with black-eyed peas and served with greens that's said to bring prosperity when served on New Year's Day, and a collard leaf pressed to the forehead is considered a home remedy for a headache. But mostly, they disappear off the plate before anyone's had a chance to do anything but enjoy their taste!

—JLL

© Chia Chong Photography

Dishing with Paula Deen

By Jessica Leigh Lebos

FOR THE FIRST LADY OF SOUTHERN COOKING, SAVANNAH WILL ALWAYS BE HOME

Find yourself at the corner of Whitaker and Congress almost any day of the year and you're bound to be standing in a crowd.

Hungry folks travel from all over the world to taste the flavors served up at The Lady & Sons — and to soak up a bit of the proprietor's famous charm.

With hoecakes, hog jowls and heaping helpings of stories and laughter, Paula Deen has brought Southern comfort food — and the city of Savannah — into the spotlight.

© Chia Chong Photography

Paula with her boys, Bobby (left) and Jamie: Television stardom and best-seller status have only brought this family closer together.

Paula Deen began her cooking career from her own kitchen in 1989 as The Bag Lady, putting together lunches that her sons, Jamie and Bobby, would deliver to local offices. One can hardly imagine this gregarious lady struggling with the fear of leaving her house that she details in her best-selling memoir, *Paula Deen: It Ain't All About the Cookin'*, but it was her years of self-healing at the stove that brought her dishes to perfection. As her business grew, she conquered her agoraphobia and opened a full-service restaurant in 1991. She moved the Lady & Sons downtown in 1996, and the accolades started racking up. The *Food Network* came calling in 2002, and Paula introduced ham salad and cheddar biscuits to the nation's palate.

These days you're more likely to catch a glimpse of Paula on the *Food Network* or smiling at you in the checkout aisle of the grocery store from the cover *Cooking with Paula Deen* than you are at the Lady & Sons, but her presence is always palpable in the warmth of the atmosphere, and of course, the down-home dishes started it all.

Though her schedule is now packed with filming, book signings and planning meetings, Paula makes no bones about the fact that family always comes first. While enjoying down time with her husband, Michael Groover, her sons and their families, she's always willing to dish about her favorite city.

With all your traveling, how often do you get home? What's your favorite part of coming home to Savannah?
Well, I'm fortunate that I get home a lot. I don't have a regular schedule, and every day of my life is different. I find out the day before what I'm doing, otherwise I'd get bogged down. This way, each day starts out fresh with a new surprise and it works out great!

I do love it every time I cross over that bridge to Wilmington Island and I look to the right and I see my house. I have a beautiful view of the marsh!

You've called Savannah home for 21 years. How has it changed?
You know, I have really seen the downtown area come to life. I was located in the Best Western on the southside of town until 1996, and I remember when I told my customers that I was going to be moving my restaurant downtown, so many of them were so fearful for me! They said, "Paula, are you sure? It's so sketchy down there!" And I said, "You know, y'all, that's where I belong. That's where my food belongs—in the middle of all that history."

Of course, Garibaldi's and Vinnie Van Go-Go's were already down there, and the more of us that took that chance to move downtown, the more the area just blossomed. It was like we gave it steroids—or just fed it well! It just started growing and making a lot of changes, with all those cool lofts and people living right there in the thick of it. My personal assistant wouldn't live anywhere else, because when you live downtown you can just walk everywhere. In fact, the only time he ever cranks up his car is to come on out to my house.

You've become an integral part of Savannah's modern history. What parts of the city's past fascinate you?
I grew up in the little town of Albany, Georgia, which I thought was the most fabulous place. Then I moved to Savannah and became friends with people who were the same age as I was and they talk about growing up in Savannah and going to Savannah High and the beaches and the old movie theaters, and I'm just a teeny bit jealous!

I like to go on the tours when I have people come down to visit with me, because it's such a good treat for them, and I always learn so much. My out-of-town company is just amazed at the history we have here. My girlfriends and I don't like to do a whole lot of walking and we like to stay cool, so we like the air-conditioned rides. Sometimes, we'll rent a horse and buggy and go out at nighttime. When you live here, you don't take the time to do things like that. You get blasé about it, but just because you live here, doesn't mean you know anything!

What are some of your personal "Don't Miss" attractions?
I love all the churches, and I always, always try to take folks to see **Cathedral of St. John the Baptist**. It's truly breathtaking, just a masterpiece.

If you have a chance, you don't want to miss **Tybee Island**. That beach town just marches to the beat of a different drum! And **Fort Pulaski** is so neat for the kids; I used to take my boys out there. And I just love the **Telfair Museum** and **Jepson Center for the Arts**.

What are your favorite activities with your grandson, Jack?
Forsyth Park is always so lovely with the fountains. They opened the café this year where you can buy refreshments. The trolley cars are special too. What child doesn't like a ride on a trolley car? His mommy and daddy take him out to the beach and all the fun places around Savannah, but when he comes my house, he says "Ginny, let's cook." He calls me "Ginny" because he couldn't' say "Granny" when he was little and it just stuck — isn't that precious? Sometimes he just wants to "pretend cook" in my bed.

Also, my husband, Michael, is a boat captain, and Jack loves riding in PeePaw's boat. He'll probably be wanting to go out on the tugboats with him soon enough!

So where do you eat when you're home?
Well, you know, I do love to cook, so we eat in most of the time. When we do go out, it's low-key. We don't tarry much away from the island. We adore **elē** on Highway 80 — it's so elegant. And we absolutely love **Sundae Café** on Tybee Island.

We often stop into **Uncle Bubba's**—and it's not just because half the restaurant is mine! I'm just so proud of my brother and his team down there. The char-grilled oysters are right there at the top, the crab stew and the shrimp and grits are just so good, but I'll tell you what, Uncle Bubba's has the best fried fish I've ever put in my mouth. And fried shrimp, and fried oysters, and the Lowcountry Boil, too!

What's the story behind the dinner bell that's rung every day at the Lady & Sons?
What better way to announce lunch? My son, Bobby, came up with the idea of ringing a bell every day at 11 o'clock and 5 o'clock so everyone would know it was time to eat. We had that bell made by

a local blacksmith here in Savannah. Nita Jones— we call her "Jellyroll" — rings it every day. She's so personable with the people, and we felt like it was right up Nita's alley to welcome everybody into the restaurant.

What is it about Southern cooking that draws people to come from far and wide to come eat?
Well, I have had the opportunity to be on TV and people hear me talking about it and I think people are just fascinated with the South. I think Southern people, we really own who we are, and it comes out in the food. Our cooking has a place in history, and part of learning about a culture is eating that region's food. Plus, it just tastes so darn good. It's simple, it's honest, it's comforting. I still have a simple palate. I would rather have a piece of fried chicken, some mashed potatoes, collard greens and a hoecake more than anything else in the world.

Every one of your cookbooks is a best-seller. What else do people need to recreate your famous dishes in their own kitchens?
Honey, you knew I was going to say plenty of butter! My type of cooking is just real simple, and I want my cookbooks to be easy for people. They just need to want to cook. I don't want people to have to hunt things down and just be able to use ingredients from the regular grocery store or what's in their pantry.

You've got to have the food, and you've also got to have the tools. Cast iron pots and frying pans are good basics. We've got a speckleware line on the market inspired by some pots that I have that must be a hundred years old. It's such a Southern look, we wanted to recreate it, but this new stuff is non-stick and I like that.

What new projects are in the works with *Food Network* and product lines?
I'm having so much fun working with my team on new products. We pretty much have products for every room of the house now—from cake mixes, spices, pork products to cookware! We also designed my furniture collection including mattresses. As you can see, we've been very busy and I love it!

Many locals remember kicking back in one of the squares with one of your sack lunches. Is there any truth to the rumor that you're reopening the Bag Lady?
You know, I think that there might be some truth to that rumor. We're still putting pencil to paper, pulling all the details together to figure out how to make it work. I doubt we could recreate the original concept, since it was my sons who originally delivered all those lunches.

Hey, but you know what you could charge for a sandwich if Bobby showed up at people's doors?
[laughs] Honey, I sold those sandwiches for so cheap back then! I was so afraid I was going to price myself out. Everything was so reasonable. The Bag Lady was great when it was my kids running the routes, but then I needed their help in the restaurant.

So this new version would be a take-out place, lighter meals that you can enjoy at your desk or in the shade somewhere. You know, just open your brown paper bag and enjoy the weather! Like I said, we're still just talking about it, but downtown in our building, I think it could be a neat, little old-timey place.

How do you describe Savannah to those who have yet to visit?
When I'm away, I'm always trying to make a picture of Savannah to people, and the same world always comes up: Magical. I can't imagine living anywhere else. I've had the opportunity to travel so much in the past few years, but my heart belongs here. It's just a beautiful, magical city, so rich in culture and history. And unlike so many other places, Savannah has managed to keep its integrity while moving forward in the modern world. It will always be my home. ✳

IT'S ALL ABOUT THE BARBECUE

Ever since humans discovered fire, folks have thrown meat over the heat and charred it to their liking. Since then, a whole lot of science and sweat has gone into developing perfect techniques and superior sauce recipes—ensuring that the Southern appetite for barbecue will never diminish.

When most folks think barbecue, they think pork. The Spanish introduced hunting wild boar to the Americas in the 1500's, but it was the Native Americans who showed them how to make it tender by burying their bounty and smoking it over a bed of coals. Nowadays, just about every kind of meat makes it to the grill. Here in Savannah, you can find almost every style of barbecue—slow-cooked, from the grill, on a bun or on the bone—made from every kind of protein: Pork, beef, chicken—and you'd better believe it—even tofu.

Of course, barbecue is as much about the meat as its dressing: In the deep South we're partial to a sweet, tomato-based sauce with a kick, while our neighbors to the north swear by their mayo and vinegar. Every barbecue joint has its own sauce with closely guarded ingredients, and deciding on your favorite barbecue restaurant is a personal process that needs time and multiple tastings.

But there's one thing on which every barbecue lover agrees: It needs to be accompanied by coleslaw. But don't get us started on how many recipes there are for that!   —JLL

© Angela Hopper Photography

dine | directory

45 Bistro | *p. 12*

B. Matthew's Eatery | *p. 20*

Belford's Seafood & Steaks | *p. 21*

Dolphin Reef Restaurant | *p. 15*

45 Bistro	**912.234.3111**	**123 E. Broughton Street**	**45bistro.com**
700 Drayton	912.721.5002	700 Drayton Street	mansiononforsythpark.com/700drayton
Alligator Soul	912.232.7899	114 Barnard Street	alligatorsoul.com
Aqua Star *(Westin Savannah Harbor)*	912.201.2085	1 Resort Drive	westinsavannah.com/aquastar
AVIA Kitchen and Lounge	912.233.2116	14 Barnard Street	aviahotels.com
B. Matthew's Eatery	**912.233.1319**	**325 E. Bay Street**	**bmatthewseatery.com**
Belford's Seafood & Steaks	**912.233.2626**	**315 W. St. Julian Street**	**belfordssavannah.com**
Blowin' Smoke BBQ	**912.231.2385**		**blowinsmokebbq.com**
Blue - A Savannah Bistro *(Savannah Marriott Riverfront)*	912.233.7722	100 General McIntosh Boulevard	marriott.com/savrf
Boar's Head Grill & Tavern	912.651.9660	1 N. Lincoln Street	boarsheadgrillandtavern.com
Broughton & Bull	912.231.8888	2 E. Broughton Street	broughtonandbull.com
Café at City Market	**912.236-7133**	**224 W. St. Julian Street**	**savannahcitymarket.com**
Café GelatOhhh	**912.234.2344**	**202 W. St. Julian Street**	**gelatohhh.com**
Café Zeum *(Jepson Center for the Arts)*	**912.790.8800**	**207 W. York Street**	**telfair.org**
Courtyard Café *(The Mulberry Inn)*	912.238.1200	601 E. Bay Street	savannahhotel.com
The Crab Shack	912.786.7009	40 Estill Hammock Road	thecrabshack.com
The DeSoto Grille *(Hilton Savannah DeSoto)*	912.443.2000	15 E. Liberty Street	desotohilton.com
Dolphin Reef Oceanfront Restaurant *(Ocean Plaza Beach Resort)*	**912.786.8400**	**1401 Strand Avenue**	**dolphinreef.com**
Elizabeth on 37th	912.236.5547	105 E. 37th Street	elizabethon37th.net
Fiddlers Crab House	**912.644.7172**	**131 W. River Street**	**fiddlerscrabhouse.com**
Garibaldi's Café	912.232.7118	315 W. Congress Street	garibaldisavannah.com
Ice Cream Etcetera	**912.239.9444**	**19 Jefferson Street**	**savannahcitymarket.com**
Jazz'd Tapas Bar	912.236.7777	52 Barnard Street	jazzdsavannah.com

John Ryan's Bistro *(Doubletree Hotel)*	912.790.7000	411 W. Bay Street	stayinsavannah.com
The Lady & Sons	**912.233.2600**	**102 W. Congress Street**	**ladyandsons.com**
Leopold's Ice Cream	912.234.4442	212 E. Broughton Street	leopoldsicecream.com
Lovin' Spoons	912.355.2723	7400 Abercorn Street	lovinspoons.com
Moon River Brewing Company	**912.447.0943**	**21 W. Bay Street**	**moonriverbrewing.com**
Noble Fare	912.443.3210	321 Jefferson Street	noblefare.com
The Olde Pink House Restaurant	912.232.4286	23 Abercorn Street	
The Pirates' House Restaurant	912.233.5757	20 E. Broad Street	thepirateshouse.com
River House Seafood	**912.234.1900**	**125 W. River Street**	**riverhouseseafood.com**
River Street Riverboat	**912.232.6404**	**9 E. River Street**	**savannahriverboat.com**
Rocks on the River *(The Bohemian Hotel)*	912.721.3900	102 W. Bay Street	bohemianhotelsavannah.com
Ruth's Chris Steak House	**912.721.4800**	**111 W. Bay Street**	**ruthschris.com**
Sapphire Grill Restaurant	912.443.9962	110 W. Congress Street	sapphiregrill.com
Shannon Vineyards	912.660.5582	4197 Savannah Highway - Sylvania	shannonvineyards.com
Shrimp Factory	**912.236.4229**	**313 E. River Street**	**theshrimpfactory.com**
Starland Café	912.443.9355	11 E. 41th Street	
Sticky Fingers Rib House	912.925.7427	7921 Abercorn Street	stickyfingers.com
Tapas by Anna	**912.236.2066**	**314 W. St. Julian Street**	**savannahcitymarket.com**
Tubby's Tank House River Street	912.233.0770	115 E. River Street	tubbysriverstreet.com
Tubby's Tank House Thunderbolt	**912.354.9040**	**2909 River Drive**	**tubbysthunderbolt.com**
Uncle Bubba's Oyster House	**912.897.6101**	**104 Bryan Woods Road**	**unclebubbas.com**
Vic's on the River	**912.721.1000**	**26 E. Bay Street**	**vicsontheriver.com**
Vinnie Van Go-Go's	**912.233.6394**	**317 W. Bryan Street**	**vinnievangogo.com**
WhistleStop Café	**912.651.3656**	**303 MLK, Jr. Boulevard**	**chsgeorgia.org**
Wild Wing Café	912.790.9464	27 Barnard Street	wildwingcafe.com
Windows *(The Hyatt Regency Savannah)*	912.238.1234	2 West Bay Street	savannah.hyatt.com

Fiddlers Crab House | *p. 5*

River House Seafood | *p. 4*

The Shrimp Factory | *p. 19*

Vic's on the River | *p. 18*

© Old Town Trolley Tours of Savannah, Inc.

© Bryan Stovall

Furniture showroom at 24e

shop|*savannah*

On the hunt for handmade crafts, hot styles and hundred year-old antiques? All can be found in Savannah's charming shopping districts, each with a personality all its own. Cruise bustling River Street to pick up souvenirs and treat yourself to a sweet and explore storied City Market for a perfect piece of art to adorn your walls at home. Dress yourself to the nines with apparel, shoes and jewelry from the boutiques on Broughton Street and decorate your abode with elegant accents from the Downtown Design District. Peruse the places in between for exquisite gifts and one-of-a-kind treasures, and if your dogs start barking (that's Southernese for sore feet), grab a ride on the ***dot*** Express Shuttle or just sit awhile with your packages on a bench in a square. It's been said that looking is half the fun; the other half is bringing home a piece of your journey that you'll cherish forever.

© Erin Adams Photography

What's in Store

BROWSE—PERHAPS TO BUY—ON A DELIGHTFUL SHOPPING SOJOURN

By Carrie J. Rodgers

In recent years, a retail explosion has left Savannah studded with boutiques that come in every size, color and style. Whether you're looking for a designer cocktail dress to wear to dinner at the **Sapphire Grill** or a souvenir with a bit more sizzle than a Bird Girl magnet, you're likely to find just what you're looking for and more. We just hope you left plenty of extra room in your suitcase.

When hunting for trends and wearable treasures, the place to start is Broughton Street. Beginning on Broughton's west end, pop into one of Savannah's most unique jewelers, **Zia**—a small boutique with big-statement jewelry from around the globe. Just a few doors down at **satchel**, working artisan Elizabeth Seeger sells her original leather purses, wallets and accessories, all crafted in her on-site workshop.

If your taste trends toward metropolitan, take in the high fashions and surreal window displays at **Marc by Marc Jacobs**. Around the corner, **Red Clover** has fun, affordable frocks and flashy accessories. All kinds of designer treasures can be found on the racks at **Cherry Picked Consignments**, and new-kid-on-the-block **fab'rik** makes the fabulous affordable in its stunning three-story space. For the finishing touch, hop over to **See Jane**, a "modern apothecary" specializing in high-end cosmetics and skin care products.

© Visit Savannah

Just around the corner on Barnard Street, you'll find two stores worth a visit: **Terra Cotta** and **Kitchens on the Square**. The former focuses on Provincial-chic apparel, beauty products and gifts, while the latter— a favorite shopping destination of celebrity chef Paula Deen—serves up a helping of fun cookware and gifts for your favorite foodie.

Back on Broughton, **BleuBelle Boutique** is a fashionista's fantasy, with racks of trendy women's apparel from designers like Diane von Furstenberg and BCBG. Across the street at **Nourish**, pamper yourself with heavenly, handmade organic soaps and bath products. Sophistication reigns at **Gaucho**, where beaded evening gowns hang next to upscale, colorful casualwear.

Work your way east to **DC2 Design**, a décor store with a dazzling window display that has lured many an unsuspecting shopper into browsing—and splurging on—the shop's luxe home goods and accessories. Neighboring **James Gunn**, a women's boutique with a deceiving name, offers a mix of both original designs and designer apparel in a distinctly Southern style.

Just across Broughton is one of Savannah's sweetest shopping spots, the **Savannah Bee Company Honey House**. Savannah Bee Company has been featured on the *Travel Channel* and in magazines like *Vogue* and *O*, and the Honey House gives shoppers a chance to sample its gorgeous artisanal honeys, honey-infused bath products and more.

The eclectic stores housed in **City Market** are too numerous to name here; the best way to discover them is to simply stroll. You'll come across painters' studios next to book shops and accessories on top of galleries. For fans of "The Lady," the **Paula Deen Store**

Opposite: Bring beauty back to the bath with handcrafted, natural products from **Nourish**. *(see ad above) Above left:* Take a break from shopping with a leisurely stroll through Factor's Walk.

is a must-shop right around the corner, stocking all manner of kitchenware, collectibles and home goods, including items from Paula's own signature collection.

Perched at the buzzing corner of Broughton and Whitaker streets is the **Paris Market & Brocante**, one of the grand dames of Savannah shopping. This two-level emporium is part antique store, part curio cabinet, and is filled from floor to ceiling with treasures plucked from around the globe, from French colognes to vintage couture to science-class anatomical models. Across the street, peruse the latest in Southern men's fashion at Savannah's premier gentlemen's clothier, **J. Parker Ltd.** Think signature seersucker suits, colorful boatwear and plenty of golf apparel.

Even if you're not in the market for fine contemporary furniture, choosy decorators should swing by **24e** to admire owner Ruel Joyner's stunning collection of "Lowcountry Modern" furnishings. It's a *bona fide* wonderland of glittering chandeliers, sumptuous fabrics and striking lines. If you're feeling overwhelmed, make use of 24e's renowned design consultation services to make your home or office space the hippest on the block. Next door and up the stairs, check out **Civvies**, an eclectic boutique where you can find new and "lightly recycled" men's and women's fashions, plus kitschy gift items.

No matter what the season, **Copper Penny** is always a step ahead with the latest collection of designer frocks, tops and jeans as well as a marvelous selection of footwear. The Charleston, SC-based boutique pays special attention to its Savannah store, offering excellent sales and unique items—fashion moves forward here at a snappy pace!

For a bit of history and a lot of bling, the venerable **Levy Jewelers** is one of Savannah's oldest downtown businesses and its most prestigious jeweler. Family-owned for four generations, Levy's sparkling inventory includes Waterford Crystal, designer watches and gemstones of every shape, color and carat. Treat your feet one block over at **Globe Shoe Co.**, which stocks both fashionable and functional high-end men's and women's shoes.

It would be easy to spend an entire day browsing Broughton Street, but there are plenty of gems to be unearthed in other corners of the Historic District. If you're searching for the perfect keepsake or funky addition to your home, you shouldn't miss **shopSCAD**. The shelves here overflow with enchanting, edgy, one-of-a-kind items, from hand-dyed velvet curtains to blown-glass salt and pepper shakers—all crafted by Savannah College of Art and Design students, alumni and faculty.

Stroll a few blocks west, beneath the canopy of Spanish moss on scenic Jones Street, until you come to Whitaker Street. Here you'll find an off-the-beaten path cluster of boutiques labeled the Downtown Design District, one of Savannah's burgeoning shopping centers.

At **James Hogan**, peruse the racks of upscale women's fashions which are lined with couture from Hogan himself, plus smart pieces from select American and European designers. Across the street at **La Paperie**, a handsome collection of stationery and journals just might inspire you to follow local literary legends like Flannery O'Connor, Conrad Aiken and John Berendt in penning the next Southern Gothic masterpiece.

While you're in the area, explore two exquisite home décor boutiques, **One Fish Two Fish**, a depot of charming bedding, furniture and books and **Arcanum**, which features antiques and unique pieces for your abode. Up the block is **Mint Boutique**, specializing in feminine frocks and cocktail gowns. Right across the street is **Custard** and its racks of edgy, modern fashion.

Like the city itself, Savannah's shops are a fusion of countless styles and influences, from Lowcountry quaint to cosmopolitan chic to art school underground. Hit the cobblestones and you'll discover a million ways to take home a slice of Savannah. After all, a good hostess never lets her guests leave empty-handed. ❁

DON'T LEAVE SAVANNAH WITHOUT

© Leopold's Ice Cream

Must-have memorabilia for your loved ones back home—or to keep for yourself.

SOMETHING OLD. Dive into Savannah's treasure trove of antique stores for estate jewelry, paintings, furnishings, rare books and charming knick-knacks. Try **Southern Antiques**, **Jere's Antiques** and the **Universal Trading Company**.

A TIN OF BENNE WAFERS. Available throughout downtown and the historic district, these sesame-flavored treats from **Byrd Cookie Company** are a gift in itself, and the collectible square tins with Savannah's most beautiful scenes last long after last buttery crumb is gone.

ORIGINAL ARTWORK. Remember your Savannah stay forever with a black-and-white aerial shot of downtown or serene watercolor of the marsh. No one can capture the majesty of your favorite scene like the local working artists of **City Market** and **shopSCAD**.

PECAN PRALINES. Pecans layered with sugar, cream and butter? Yes, please. Score a free sample from **Savannah's Candy Kitchen** or **River Street Sweets**; you won't be able to resist a box. These crunchy treats don't melt in the heat, which makes them a perfect souvenir to share with the folks back home.

HOMEMADE ICE CREAM. Of course, it would take some planning, but taking home a pint or two of **Leopold's** ice cream is worth the double-packed cooler. Carefully crafted in custom-made batches since 1919, Leopold's is a straight-up Savannah tradition, offering one-of-a-kind flavors like Chocolate Chewies 'n' Cream, Girl Scouts Thin Mints 'n' Cream and the famous Tutti-Frutti.

SWEET TEA. Recreate the city's favorite beverage at home with the iced tea blend from the **Savannah Tea Room**—the peach version will quench your thirst 'til your next trip. All you need is a bucket of ice, a bit of sugar (well, maybe a bunch) and a tall glass.

A TASTE O' HONEY. The bees stay busy with all the flowers of the Lowcountry to create some of the most amazing artisanal honey in the world: Take home a few bottles—as well as honeycombs and body products—from the **Savannah Bee Company** to prolong the sweet memories.

A COPY OF SAVANNAH: A SOUTHERN JOURNEY. Love the articles, photos and fun facts found in this book? The copy you have in your hands is the property of your hotel, but you can take home your own for $19.99. Consult your concierge for details. —JLL

MORNING TO MIDNIGHT
RENAISSANCE

NO MATTER WHAT THE HOUR, IT'S ALWAYS BUSTLING IN CITY MARKET

by Laura Clark

Savannah is a city of personalities. A visit will reveal not only the typically warm-hearted nature of its locals, but also the distinct dispositions of the city's historic neighborhoods. Jones Street, with its exquisite facades and towering oaks is like a genteel older woman, continually whispering stories of the past. River Street, home to festivals and late-night revelers is a boisterous fun-lover, always looking for a reason to celebrate. And then there is City Market, the Renaissance Man, many different things to different people and a friend to all.

Spanning nearly two blocks on West Bryan Street between Barnard and Montgomery Streets, City Market offers something for nearly everyone. First class restaurants dot the area, mingled with unique shops and art galleries and bars that come alive each evening with locals and tourists alike. The friendly energy, the bustling shops, the diners enjoying leisurely meals indoors or at tables lining the two large outdoor courtyards—this is only the most modern chapter in City Market's long history as a place that brings people together.

Established in the early 1700's as Savannah's commercial and social center, the Market was once home to merchants of all kinds and even served as a makeshift hospital during the Civil War's Siege of Savannah.

Two large structures were destroyed by fire before 1872, after which an ornate brick building was erected where Ellis Square now sits. Boasting large windows and a 50-foot roofline, this iconic Market building stood until 1954, when it was torn down to make room for a parking garage. The loss of this historic structure helped to ignite Savannah's nationally recognized historic preservation movement, and private investors acted in recent decades to restore City Market to its former glory.

Today, the market offers comfort and respite to all. The two-block pedestrian mall offers benches, shade, chairs and tables for a rest, since getting around City Market is easiest on foot. Several tour companies start and end their tours in the intersection of Jefferson and St. Julian Streets, the heart of the pedestrian area. Despite its seemingly small reach, there is so much to do in City Market that an entire, perfect day could be spent on its streets.

In the Morning
Once you've fueled up for the morning, head down to the corner of West Bryan and Jefferson Streets for a look at Savannah's beloved horse-drawn carriages and a chat with the tour guides who drive them. Friendly and knowledgeable, these folks will answer any question you have about the Market or Savannah in general, and the kids will love to pet the sweet-tempered horses. Those looking to venture out of the neighborhood for a leisurely tour of the city should certainly consider a carriage tour. Savannah's colorful history revealed by the guides and the clip-clop of hooves on brick-paved streets will help to take you back in time.

From the carriages, move down to **The Art Center at City Market**. Here, art lovers of all ages will enjoy watching local artists creating masterpieces in individual studio spaces. Hours may be spent meandering down the halls to view—and have the chance to buy—art ranging from paintings, sculpture and glass to jewelry and fabric art.

After Lunch
Seek out a light lunchtime nosh at a City Market staple, **Tapas by Anna**. This eatery boasts big flavors and plenty of outdoor seating with an excellent view for people-watching. Take advantage of Savannah's coastal positioning with one of Anna's many seafood dishes, including bacon-wrapped scallops, or go for the burger seasoned with Cajun spices. Nearly everyone will find something they like here.

Be sure to eat enough to have energy for an active afternoon of shopping and gallery hopping, for City Market is one of the best places in Savannah for both. Store-weary spouses and thrifty tourists need not worry; the Market boasts a varied retail community, and fun can be had by spending more time than money.

The **Savannah Candy Kitchen** is housed in the former location of Sweet Georgia Brown's, the piano bar made famous in *Midnight in the Garden of Good and Evil*, and is a must for any sweet tooth. Free samples and candy-making demonstrations abound, as do overflowing barrels of treats and trays of the

There is so much to do in City Market that an entire, perfect day could be spent on its streets.

© Bryan Stovall

© City Market

© City Market

© Bryan Stovall

Above top: Dine indoors or out at **Belford's Seafood and Steaks**. *(see ad - page 21) Above bottom:* Grab a slice at **Vinnie Van Go-Go's**, situated on one of the busiest corners in town. *Opposite:* **Wild Wing Café** is the place to enjoy Savannah's fine weather, listen to some live music, or watch your favorite team on one of multiple TV's.

city's famed pecan pralines. If sugar isn't your thing, **Twinkle** down the block offers eye-candy for jewelry lovers. Be sure to stop by **All Things Georgia** for Peach State-related gifts.

Those in search of a bit of culture should head to the area's assorted art galleries. At the wonderfully offbeat **A.T. Hun Art Gallery** you'll find the *Big Lebowski*-inspired paintings of owner Chuck Hamilton (often seen deftly playing the keyboard in the corner) as well as the paintings of other local artists. For the more traditionally-minded, the **Thomas Kinkade City Market Gallery** holds a large collection of local landscape compositions from the nationally known artist.

At the end of your busy afternoon, seek respite in the newly restored **Ellis Square**, where shaded café tables and benches beckon weary travelers. For kids sticky from the day's activities, a playful interactive fountain is nearly irresistible. Bring a bath-

ing suit for rowdy water-lovers but the more conservative puddle-jumpers will be fine without. The square also plays host to a visitor center and public bathrooms and is a great home base for any Market tourist.

Into the Night

Once the sun begins to set, City Market reinvents itself as the cool older brother of its daytime personality. Embrace this party-loving vibe by grabbing the best—and possibly biggest—slice of pizza in town at the casual and laid back **Vinnie Van Go-Go's**. For a more formal dinner, head across the courtyard to **Belford's Savannah Seafood and Steaks**, where a refined atmosphere and varied menu makes it a favorite of many.

Before you hit the bars, don't forget dessert. Stop in at **Café GelatOhhh** for an icy treat of artisan-style gelato made into decadently unique flavors with fresh ingredients. Can't choose between Bananas Fosters or Honeycomb Crunch or just too full for an entire serving? The staff will be happy to provide tastes of any flavor available.

Now that your belly is full, it's time to hit the bars. For an all-around friendly atmosphere, drop by **Pour Larry's**. With an evolving roster of live music acts, DJ's, beer pong and poker nights, this watering hole is sure to host energetic crowds.

Perhaps the perfect way to end the day is to grab a table at **Wild Wing Café**, one of downtown's most spirited late-night establishments. Once you've grabbed a drink, found a breezy outdoor table, leaned back in your chair and enjoyed the live music, ,here is the moment to reflect upon your City Market day.

You've experienced a wealth of art, culture, history and dining—all in the space of two blocks. ❀

© City Market

© City Market

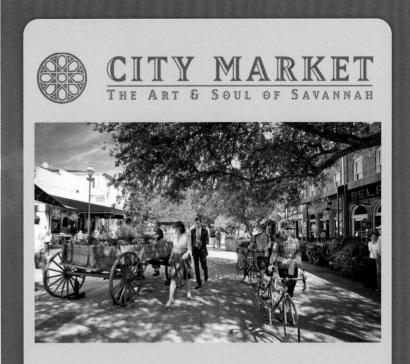

Map labels:

HARBOR ST.

GENERAL MCINTOSH BLVD.

E. BROAD ST.

E. BAY ST.

Washington Square

E. CONGRESS ST.

E. ST. JULIAN ST.

Warren Square

HOUSTON ST.

PRICE ST.

Emmet Park

E. BRYAN ST.

Reynolds Square

HABERSHAM ST.

LINCOLN ST.

ABERCORN ST.

DRAYTON

U.S. Customs House

Johnson Square

BULL ST.

RIVER ST.

Olympic Torch

Waving Girl

Factor's Walk

E. BAY ST.

City Hall

dottie Streetcar

Historic Wharf

RIVER ST.

Rousakis Plaza

Cotton Exchange

River Queen

Georgia Queen

Savannah International Trade & Convention Center

Hutchinson Island

1 2 3 4 5 6 7 8 9 10 11 12

A B C D E F G H

River Street

This cobblestoned stretch is a favorite place to pick up a perfect souvenir, enjoy a sumptuous meal, watch a taffy pull or hop on *dottie* for a free streetcar ride to explore more than 100 shops, restaurants and pubs. Here's a host of facts about Savannah's riverfront you may not know:

Map illustration by Michael Karpovage (KarpovageCreative.com) ©2011

 It's a multicultural wonderland. Throughout the year, River Street hosts family-friendly festivals from **Oktoberfest**, featuring *leiderhosen* and wiener dog races, to **Fiesta Latina** and its swinging salsa music and spicy cuisine. And of course, there's the largest **St. Patrick's Day** celebration in the country, when everyone becomes Irish for the day just for showing up.

 You can sit with history—literally. Nestled above the river level on Yamacraw Bluff on the property of the **Hyatt Regency Savannah** is a Mediterranean-style, rounded white bench created by the Colonial Dames in 1905 to mark the exact spot (D-12) General Oglethorpe pitched his tent to rest his first night after docking in the new colony on February 12, 1733.

 The night sky crackles with color regularly. Fireworks elicit "oohs" and "aahs" every first Friday of the month when **Savannah Riverfront** puts on a fabulous show of pyrotechnics and live music. Artisans line the plaza with their distinctive works, and many shops stay open late on **First Fridays**. **First Saturdays** are all-day events centered around artisans lining Rousakis Plaza (D-9) with their distinctive works; the festivals feature family entertainment, juried arts and crafts, novelty food items and often contests.

 The nation's fourth largest port lies just up the river. The **Georgia Ports Authority** handles more than 2.5 million shipping containers from all over the world, and many of the goods that hit everyone's favorite stores around the country passed through Savannah first. Find out more about how Savannah plays into the global shipping economy at *gaports.com* and **The Savannah Port Journal** website, *savannahportjournal.com*.

 The city's finest music plays under the moonlight. In the middle of spring, **Fine Arts on the River** invites visitors and locals to enjoy classical music at no charge from the likes of the Savannah Winds Symphony and great grooves from Cajun, mariachi and other types of musicians. When the bands take a break, DJ's spin jazz and blues to keep the mood swingin'!

The ends of the earth are under your feet. Savannah's early developers recycled the ballast used on ships to pave the streets, laying cobblestones originally quarried in Canada, the British Isles, France, Spain and beyond. Still solid—and charming—after almost three centuries, the varied materials of River Street (as well as some of the retaining walls and structures) include limestone, granite, quartz and basalt.

The public transit runs on fried shrimp. Well, not *exactly*. The city's *dot* system's brought together green technology with local ingenuity when it retrofitted 1930s streetcar called *dottie* (D-6) to run on biodiesel fuel comprised partly of used vegetable oil from River Street restaurants. So go ahead, have another basket of crispy shrimp or oysters—it's for a good cause!

Pirates once docked on these shores. Lore has it that sea-faring outcasts and plunderers—including the fearsome Bluebeard—made liberal use of Savannah's old inns and pubs in the 18th and 19th centuries. The old tunnel at the **Pirate's House Restaurant** (B-3) emptied out near the river, where unsuspecting sailors plied with rum were shanghaied onto waiting vessels and forced into pirate life.

Docking didn't come easy. The high bluff made for good anchorage for early ships, but the steep bank and treacherous currents proved challenging for loading and unloading passengers and supplies in the city's early days. Savannah's wharves benefitted from the Industrial Revolution when equipment powerful enough to drive concrete piles into the river bottom was brought in, creating easy access for large vessels. You can still see the public wharf towards the east end (D-7), constructed in 1872 for smaller boats.

Shopping hasn't changed much in a few hundred years. You can peruse the wares of more than a hundred merchants within the shady open-air market at the east end (D-5) of River Street's shopping district, just like Savannah shoppers did when this road was little more than a bumpy route. (Though 18th-century housewives could never have imagined the fun, color-changing solar technology found at **Del Sol**!) Today's shopkeepers still sweep the sidewalks in front of historic warehouses, though the spaces inside are now air-conditioned havens.

Check *riverstreetsavannah.com* for a full schedule of events!

shop | directory

24e | p. 34

Art Center at City Market | p. 89

Blue Belle

Custard

24e	**912.233.2274**	**24 E. Broughton Street**	**24estyle.com**
37th @ Abercorn Antiques	912.233.0064	201 E. 37th Street	37aad.com
All Things Georgia	**912.233.7017**	**305 W. St. Julian Street**	**savannahcitymarket.com**
Arcanum	912.236.6000	422 Whitaker Street	arcanumsavannah.com
BleuBelle Boutique	912.443.0011	205 W. Broughton Street	bleubelle.com
Byrd Cookie Company	912.355.1716	6700 Waters Avenue	byrdcookiecompany.com
Cinnamon Bear	**912.232.2888**	**309 W. St. Julian Street**	**savannahcitymarket.com**
Copper Penny	912.629.6800	22 W. Broughton Street	shopcopperpenny.com
Custard Boutique	912.232.4733	414 Whitaker Street	custardboutique.com
DC2 Design	912.233.2870	109 W. Broughton Street	dc2design.com
Del Sol Savannah	**912.236.6622**	**423 E. River Street**	**delsol.com**
E. Shaver Bookseller	912.234.7257	326 Bull Street	
Gaucho	912.234.7414	18 E. Broughton Street	gauchosav.com
Globe Shoe Co.	912.232.8161	17 E. Broughton Street	
J. Parker Ltd.	912.234.0004	19 W. Broughton Street	jparkerltd.com
James Gunn	912.790.7500	112 W. Broughton Street	jamesgunnonline.com
James Hogan	912.234.0374	412 Whitaker Street B	jameshogan.com
Jere's Antiques	912.236.2815	9 N. Jefferson Street	jeresantiques.com
Kathi Rich	912.236.7424	2515 Abercorn Street	kathirich.com
Kitchens on the Square	912.236.0100	38 Barnard Street	kitchensonthesquare.com
La Paperie	912.443.9349	409 Whitaker Street	lapaperie.net
Levy Jewelers	912.233.1163	101 E. Broughton Street	levyjewelers.com
Marc by Marc Jacobs	912.234.2800	322 W. Broughton Street	marcjacobs.com
Meinhardt Winery	**912.644.7200**	**306 W. St. Julian Street**	**meinhardtvineyards.com**

Mint Boutique	912.341.8961	413 Whitaker Street	mintsavannah.com
Nature's Treasures	**912.234.1238**	**213 W. St. Julian Street**	**savannahcitymarket.com**
Nourish	**912.232.3213**	**202 W. Broughton Street**	**nourishsavannah.com**
One Fish Two Fish	912.447.4600	401 Whitaker Street	onefishstore.com
Paris Market & Brocante	912.232.1500	36 W. Broughton Street	theparismarket.com
Paula Deen Store	912.232.1579	108 W. Congress Street	pauladeen.com
Red Clover	912.236.4053	53 Montgomery Street	shopredclover.com
River Street Sweets	912.233.6220	13 E. River Street	riverstreetsweets.com
Satchel	912.233.1008	311 W. Broughton Street	shopsatchel.com
The Savannah Bee Company	912.233.7873	104 W. Broughton Street	savannahbee.com
Savannah Cigars	**912.233.2643**	**308 W. Congress Street**	**savannahcigarsinc.com**
Savannah Prose and Poetry	**912.224.7427**	**309 W. St. Julian Street**	**savannahcitymarket.com**
Savannah Shoe Co.	912.232.2334	226 W. Broughton Street	savannahshoeco.com
Savannah Tea Room	912.239.9690	7 E. Broughton Street	savannahtearoom.com
Savannah's Candy Kitchen	912.233.5411	225 E. River Street	savannahcandy.com
Savannah's Candy Kitchen	912.201.9501	318 W. St. Julian Street	savannahcandy.com
Scents of Savannah	**912.447.1817**	**33 Jefferson Street**	**savannahcitymarket.com**
See Jane	912.234.1080	323 W. Broughton Street	seejaneshop.com
shopSCAD	912.525.5180	340 Bull Street	shopscadonline.com
Silver Silk and Beads	**912.236.2890**	**310 W. St. Julian Street**	**savannahcitymarket.com**
Southern Charm Antiques	912.233.9797	250 Bull Street	southerncharmantiques.com
Terra Cotta	912.236.6150	34 Barnard Street	
Trolley Stop Gifts	**912.233.5604**	**217 W. St. Julian Street**	**savannahcitymarket.com**
Twinkle	**912.234.1001**	**307 W. Bryan Street**	**savannahcitymarket.com**
Universal Trading	912.233.1585	27 Montgomery Street	
ZIA	912.233.3237	325 W. Broughton Street	ziaboutique.com

Del Sol | *p. 30*

Nourish | *p. 33*

Paula Deen Store

River Street | *p. 83*

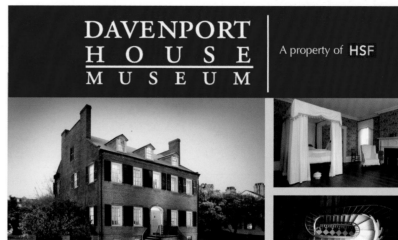
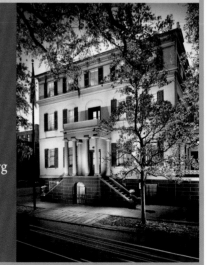
44

Old Town Trolley tour viewing the historic Kehoe House

explore | *savannah*

a guide to the grid | **small city, big faith** | **get around town** | **savannah's stars** | **above the door and behind the curtains** | **a day at the beach** | **take it outside**

From the moment General Oglethorpe declared it a colony of England in 1733, this sunny spot on the bluff has claimed its place in our nation's narrative. Once a prosperous trading post operated by the Yamacraw Tribe, Georgia's first city played prominent roles in both the Revolutionary and Civil Wars, served as a pirate haven , was the birthplace of Methodism and the Girl Scouts of America, inspired the classic tune "Jingle Bells" and the entire repertoire of Johnny Mercer, and has hosted Civil Rights movement heroes and Olympic athletes. Every street corner and edifice has at least one tale to tell, and even the dead get to have their say. Savannah takes its responsibility to the past mighty seriously, but that doesn't mean our history lessons aren't a good time. As you amble down the cobblestone streets or enjoy the slow ride of a trolley tour along the squares, we invite you to soak up Savannah's many stories—and make some memories of your own.

A Guide to the Grid

LONG AGO, GENERAL OGLETHORPE FIGURED OUT THAT IT'S HIP TO BE SQUARE

By Laura Clark

There is perhaps no better way to enjoy Savannah than to tour its squares. Be it by foot, trolley, pedicab or car, a look between the azalea-lined paths of these communal public spaces presents a colorful view of both the city's past and present.

Once upon a time, there was a coastal bluff above a river that flowed steadily towards the Atlantic Ocean. But starting in 1733, when General James Oglethorpe arrived on the scene to build a colony in the name of England's King George II, this area forty feet above the water would be trans-

formed into one of the world's most beautiful cities, thanks in no small part to its unique layout.

Oglethorpe, along with planner William Bull of South Carolina, designed Savannah to include more green open space than any other city in history. They established squares—plots of land reserved as public parks—amongst thriving neighborhoods of both public buildings and homes.

Today, Savannah's 24 squares act as the city's living room, offering locals and tourists alike a shady

© Bryan Stovall

Today, Savannah's 24 squares act as the **city's living room**, offering locals and tourists alike a shady venue for everything from morning coffee to concerts to holiday celebrations.

© Kevin Nightingale

venue for everything from morning coffee to concerts to holiday celebrations. So get out your cameras and lace up your shoes—Savannah's squares are waiting to be enjoyed.

Washington Square. Nearly in sight of the Savannah River, Washington Square (named after America's first president) is bright and sunny and boasts an impressive array of tulips and daffodils in the spring. In the early 1900s, the locale was the primary staging area for huge New Year's Eve bonfires and was long known to locals as "Firehouse Square" thanks to a once-neighboring station.

Warren Square. Bordered by subdued clapboard houses in neutral hues, this square was named for Revolutionary War hero and Battle of Bunker Hill casualty Continental Army General Joseph Warren and is just the place to stop for a spot of shade on the your way to the river.

Reynolds Square. Near bustling Broughton Street, Reynolds Square offers everything needed for a perfect evening out. On one end you'll find the historic and sparkling **Lucas Theatre** built in 1921, diagonally across from a stunning structure dating back to 1771, the **Olde Pink House**, still a favorite fine dining institution. And if the night's revelry has you in need of some moral alignment, look no further than the center of the square, where a monument stands to John Wesley, the founder of Methodism and a one-time rector of **Savannah Christ Church**.

Johnson Square. This sprawling spot of land by the city's gilded capitol building is host to an obelisk dedicated to General Nathanael Greene. In 1901, the Revolutionary War hero's body was removed from nearby **Colonial Park Cemetery** and re-interred beneath the monument—so be sure to tip your hat to one of Georgia's great defenders as you pass.

Opposite: While sitting in **Chippewa Square**, you may find yourself wondering how life is like a box of chocolates. *Above left:* It's only a short walk to the river from **Washington Square**. *Above:* **Johnson Square** near City Hall hosts large celebrations and pays tribute to Revolutionary War hero Nathanael Greene.

Top: Visitors pass by the **First African Baptist Church** on **Franklin Square** during a tour from **Old Town Trolley Tours** *(see ads – pages 25, 53, 69) Bottom:* The historic **Savannah Theatre** is one of America's oldest operating live theaters and offers a year-round calendar of peformances that combine music, dancing and a healthy dose of comedy. *(see ad - page 72)*

Ellis Square. It wasn't long ago that Ellis Square was but a parking lot for downtown day-trippers, but following an extensive construction project that moved the lot underground and out of sight, the square is a revitalized and renewed showcase. The new festive fountains provide a wet place to play by day and a colorful light show at night, and this friendly space is presided over by a statue dedicated to lyrical legend Johnny Mercer.

Franklin Square. Named for founding father Benjamin Franklin, this square sits next to **Vinnie Van Go-Go's**, one of the city's favorite locales for a sizable slice of New York-style pizza. At one time housing the city's water tank, Franklin Square is now home to a monument honoring the Haitian volunteer soldiers that helped defend the city during the Revolutionary War's Siege of Savannah.

Liberty Square. At one time the size of its neighboring parks, renovations to nearby Montgomery Street made Liberty Square one of the two squares that are reduced in size and stature—but stop by throughout spring to see a rainbow of blooming azaleas.

Telfair Square. This square is named for three-time Georgia Governor Edward Telfair and his daughters, Mary and Margaret. In 1886, the Telfair family opened their home to the public as an art museum and school, which continue to thrive on the edge of the square. Be sure to stop by neighboring **Jepson Center for the Arts** for excellent exhibitions of 20th and 21st century art.

Wright Square. In the heart of beautiful Bull Street, Wright Square is bordered by charming court houses and boasts a monument to Central of Georgia Railroad founder and Savannahian William W. Gordon. The square also has a memorial to Yamacraw Indian Chief and friend of the colonists, Tomochichi. Remember to tread lightly here: this locale was the first cemetery of Georgia's colonists, who were unable to move the bodies of their beloveds after establishing new sacred grounds.

Oglethorpe Square. Named after the founder of the colony of Georgia, Oglethorpe Square has plenty of benches, making it the perfect place to get a lasting look at the façade of the **Owens Thomas House**, one of the city's most exquisite house museums.

Columbia Square. With tall, pruned bushes and an ornate fountain at its center, Columbia Square is as elegant as the expansive homes and buildings that surround it, which include the **Kehoe House**, an opulent (and reportedly haunted) inn, and the **Isaiah Davenport House Museum**.

Greene Square. Quiet and lush with tall trees and subtle landscaping, this mostly residential square is adjacent to two unique and antique crooked little houses—see if you can spy them.

Crawford Square. In a primarily residential neighborhood, Crawford Square brings locals outdoors with an appealing gazebo and basketball courts. Be sure to stop by neighboring **Colonial Park Cemetery**, among the oldest burial grounds in the country and the final resting place of Button Gwinnett, one of the only signers of the Declaration of Independence to meet a violent end.

Chippewa Square. Some may know this busy Bull Street setting as "Forrest Gump Square" since its eastern end was indeed the location of the bench scenes of the Academy Award®-winning movie. Bordered by the bright lights of the historic **Savannah Theatre**, where professional singers and dancers perform family-friendly musical shows, and the perfectly pleasant **Gallery Espresso** coffee house, the square is centered around a statue of General Oglethorpe keeping watch over all that happens here.

Orleans Square. Accented gracefully by the bubbling German Memorial Fountain, Orleans Square commemorates the War of 1812 victory of the Battle of New Orleans and is within sight of the **Savannah Civic Center**.

Elbert Square. Like Liberty Square, Elbert Square is no longer possessing of the size or glory of its former years, but the stretch of land that remains is a perfect place for a rest before or after an evening spent at the nearby Civic Center.

Pulaski Square. Tall trees with outspread branches create a delightful canopy affect in quiet Pulaski Square, named for Count Casimir Pulaski, who perished during the Revolutionary War's Siege of Savannah.

Madison Square. As a busy tourist favorite, Madison Square gracefully brings the past and present together with its historic bordering buildings. The **Greene-Meldrim House** hosted General Sherman's headquarters when the Union Army took the Savannah during the Civil War. Nearby is the popular **Sorrel-Weed House**, thought to be highly haunted and offering tours daily. And be sure not to pass up the city's finest little bookshop, **E. Shaver Booksellers**, situated behind the **Hilton Savannah DeSoto Hotel**.

Lafayette Square. In the splendid shadow of the **Cathedral of St. John the Baptist** and enhanced by a refreshing fountain, Lafayette Square is the perfect place to be on a lazy Sunday afternoon. Close to the **Andrew Low House Museum** (former home to Juliette Gordon Low, founder of the Girl Scouts), this square is also within sight of the exquisite **Hamilton Turner Inn**, which was the first home in Savannah to boast electricity.

Troup Square. Bordered by closely trimmed hedges and containing an large sphere with heavenly symbols known as an "astrolabe", Troup Square is also home to the **Unitarian Universalist Church of Savannah**, known as "The Jingle Bells Church," where former organist John Pierpont, Jr. is thought to have composed the beloved holiday tune in 1857.

Whitfield Square. Quiet and romantic, this square's simple white gazebo and surrounding ornate Victorian houses make Whitfield Square a favorite wedding location for locals and visitors.

Calhoun Square. The income from Savannah's early 1800s cotton exports allowed Savannahians to build impressive houses along this shady square, which is situated next to the dazzling and imposing **Wesley Monumental Church**. If you're a fan of John Berendt's *Midnight in the Garden of Good and Evil* (or the accompanying film) be sure to stop into the nearby **"The Book" Gift Shop**.

Monterey Square. As one of Savannah's most photographed locations, Monterey Square is home to the infamous Mercer House, the main setting of the all-too true *Midnight in the Garden of Good and Evil*. After peeking inside this literary locale on one of the home's daily tours, venture across the park to see the Gothic-style **Congregation Mickve Israel** which, founded in 1733, houses one of the oldest Jewish congregations in America.

Chatham Square. Close to Forsyth Park and discreetly residential, Chatham Square (named for William Pitt, the Earl of Chatham and British Prime Minister) is hugged by Greek revival homes that transport square sitters to another time. ❋

Top: Laid out in 1837, **Madison Square** is named for the fourth President of the United States, James Madison. *Bottom:* A monument to General Casimir Pulaski is in the center of **Monterey Square**, and an unknown Revolutionary soldier is said to bured underneath.

© Kevin Nightingale

Small City, Big Faith

SAVANNAH'S SPIRITUAL LEGACY

Savannah's first church service took place the very day General Oglethorpe docked his ship at the Yamacraw Bluff on February 12, 1733. It was attended by 120 new colonists and conducted by the general himself. Since then, Savannah's spiritual legacy has only gotten stronger and more storied.

That first service had roots in the Anglican Church, and Yamacraw Indian Chief Tomochichi was so inspired by it that he traveled to England with Oglethorpe to convert to Christianity. A young Anglican priest named John Wesley was sent by the Archbishop of Canterbury as a missionary to the new colony, and after a tumultuous attempt at counseling the colonists and native tribes, he returned to London in 1738. He famously founded the Methodist movement soon after.

As declared by General Oglethorpe, the colony of Georgia was established with the promise that any religion could be practiced—with the exception of Catholicism, a defense to the threat of then Spanish-occupied Florida. A few months after the colony's establishment, the English ship *William & Sarah* brought a group of 41 Jewish travelers, mostly of Portuguese origin, to Savannah. They became the **Congregation Mickve Israel**, still operating as the third-oldest congregation in the nation and occupying one of the country's only Gothic synagogues on Monterey Square.

Around the same time a few miles further north, the community of Ebenezer was established by 300 German-speaking Lutherans who came seeking religious refuge from their home country. The Salzburgers found freedom and as well as agronomic success, and their **Jerusalem Church** in Rincon stands as the oldest continuing Lutheran congregation in the country that still uses its original edifice.

Savannah is also home to America's oldest African American church, though two lay claim to the distinction: Both **First African Baptist Church** and **First Bryan Baptist Church** trace

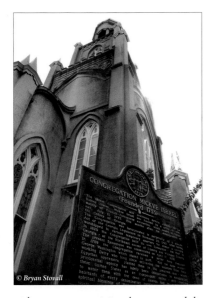

© Bryan Stovall

their roots back to Andrew Bryan, a baptized slave who founded the first ordained black Baptist church in 1788. Following a schism over religious doctrine in 1832, the congregation split, with one group retaining the name and the other claiming the original building. The first white Baptist church was established in 1800, and the majority of churches in Savannah are affiliated with some type of Baptist denomination.

By 1799, the ban on Catholicism was lifted when the city granted permission for the construction of **St. John the Baptist**, back then a small church built to accommodate Savannah's increasing population of Irish immigrants. The stunning cathedral that stands today on Bull Street was dedicated in 1876.

The late 1800s saw the advent of a revival period that brought new religious interpretations such as Christian Science, Unitarianism and Mormonism, all of whom established local communities. The Jehovah's Witness and Pentecostal movements also found homes in Savannah during this time. Two new synagogues were also organized at the turn of the century, **B'nai B'rith Jacob** and **Agudath Achim**.

The 20th century filled in any gaps in Savannah's roster of religious diversity. Large evangelical Christian congregations like **Savannah Christian Church** now thrive, as well as smaller groups practicing the traditions of Quakerism, Hindu, Buddhism and the Baha'i Faith. Savannah also has two mosques, the **Islamic Center of Savannah** and the **Masjid Jihad**.

Oglethorpe's vision of tolerance is a reality in Savannah. Not only do so many different faiths worship peacefully and respectfully, there is constant crossover of interfaith activities and support. Whatever you believe or whether you believe at all, there's no denying such a remarkable example of religious freedom. ❀   —JLL

GET AROUND TOWN

No need to reinvent the wheel with so many tour and transportation options.

By Jessica Leigh Lebos

Whether you arrived via jet plane at Savannah-Hilton Head International Airport, rolled in on the highway or sailed in by boat, we extend our warmest welcomes. As nice as your hotel room may be, you didn't come to Savannah to spend your whole time in there, right? Let's get you out the door and onto the streets!

© Bryan Stovall

© Bryan Stovall

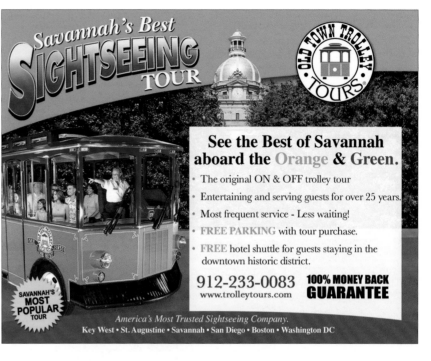

Even if you've been to Savannah before, it's always helpful to engage the services of a seasoned tour guide. For an open-air ride that hits all the important historical points from downtown through the historic district, hop on an orange and green trolley from **Old Town Trolley Tours**, in the tour business for over 25 years. The city's other trolley companies also offer excellence and experience: **Old Savannah Tours** (white) or **Oglethorpe Trolley Tours** (blue). Each has its own starting point and convenient parking lot and offer general Savannah tours as well as ghost tours, pirate tours, beach excursions and specialty services—there are so many stories in this city, you'll never hear them all!

Slow down the pace with a horse-and-carriage ride through the historic district. Your talented driver can steer a stallion while expounding on the architectural details of the homes and churches on the squares. Riding at a clip-clop pace is a memorable and romantic way to reflect on the gracious homes of a by-gone era. **Plantation Carriage Co.** and **Historic Savannah Carriage Tours** have convenient downtown pick-up spots.

If you feel like going it on your own, be sure to check out Savannah's no-fare transportation system known as the **dot**. Utilizing air-conditioned shuttles, a historic streetcar and charming ferryboats, the **dot** is a public-private partnership designed to maximize everyone's experience of Savannah and is committed to full access to riders with disabilities, in accordance with evolving ADA Accessibility Guidelines.

© Savannah Mobility Management, Inc.

Opposite: Cross the Savannah River in style in one of the fare-free **Savannah Belles** ferries. *Above left:* Imagine yourself in the days of yore while taking in the sites from a horse-drawn carriage. *Above:* The city's fare-free **dot** system includes sleek air-conditioned Exrpress Shuttles and **dottie**, a refurbished streetcar that runs on recycled vegetable oil.

Come on and take a free ride: Hop on and hop off the Express Shuttle from any of ten stops in Savannah's beautiful Historic District, including the Visitors' Center and adjoining parks. The *dot* Express Shuttle runs seven days a week, 11 am to 9 pm with less than a 20-minute wait between shuttles. Hours are often expanded to accommodate festivals and special events; please check *connectonthedot.com* for the latest information.

Thursdays through Sundays, from noon to 8pm and during special events, catch *dottie*, an authentic streetcar that runs along Historic River Street. Riding the rails, you'll pass rows of 19th-century cotton warehouses with iron catwalks from the era of King Cotton. People often make one pass down River Street as a look-see, then travel back in the opposite direction to explore any of the seven stations that fit their fancy. The one-mile track runs between Montgomery Street and the Waving Girl Landing at the east end, and the stops line up with our squares up on the bluff. *dottie* herself was manufactured in Melbourne, Australia in the 1930s, and is retrofitted with environmentally-friendly green technology: She runs on biodiesel culled from local restaurant grease. So please, keep eating up hush-puppies and plates of fried shrimp so *dottie* can keep clanging for a long, long time!

While near the river you may notice that Savannah does indeed have one of the world's busiest ports. When you're ready to cross over to the other side, share the waters with those enormous shipping vessels on a free ferryboat ride across the river on one of the *dot* system's **Savannah Belles**, named for the many prominent women in Savannah's history. Reminiscent of passenger vessels of a century ago, the Belles operate seven days a week, 7a.m. to midnight with departures and arrivals every 20-25 minutes. Board a Belle from River Street at City Hall Landing below City Hall or at Waving Girl Landing on the east end of River Street to catch a ride to Hutchison Island and the activities around the **Savannah International Trade & Convention Center** and the **Westin Savannah Harbor Golf Resort & Spa**.

If you're looking to spend some more time on the water, book a ticket with the **River Street Riverboat Company**. Each cruise is an evening of fine dining, captivating entertainment and a tour of Savannah from a unique perspective. Special holiday cruises and charters are available.

Looking for small-engine adventure? That's how they roll at **Segway of Savannah**, where you can rent a two-wheeled stand-up device that combines historic touring with the cutting edge. Add a European flair to your ride by choosing your favorite color from a fleet of über-cool Vespa mopeds available to rent from **Vespa Savannah**.

Want something more fitting to your unique tastes? If you're seeking high-style to tour the town, find yourself a top-down classic Cadillac from **Classic Caddy Tours** with seats as big as couches. And if you like your ride spooky, there are tricked-out hearses for nocturnal excursions to Savannah's most haunted nooks and crannies with **Hearse Ghost Tours Savannah**.

Prefer people-powered transportation? The three-wheeled buggies of **Savannah Pedicab** accommodate two people at a time for a breezy jaunt. Part bike, part modern rickshaw, these environmentally-responsible ways to roll are a favorite among bar-hoppers. The hipster pedal-pushers are happy to take you a few blocks or on a thorough tour up to **Forsyth Park**. You can usually find one for hire at the intersection of Bull and Broughton, or book one in advance. Of course you can power your own bike—**The Bicycle Link** on MLK, Jr. Boulevard has all the gear you need if you want to put your own feet to the pedals for a morning or an entire week.

There's bound to be some of you who'd rather use the two feet you were born with to get around. Savannah is regularly named one of the best walking cities in America, and you only need to stroll for a couple of yards to figure out why—it's flat, mostly shady and there's always something to see. Hiring a licensed guide from the many walking tour companies gets you to the best places with all the best tales—you might even try two or even three walking tours, since each one is unique to the local character in charge. For a specialized experience, try **The Savannah Walks** and its "Tours for the Educated Traveler" and **Sixth Sense Savannah**, offering spooky nighttime promenades. Just make sure to wear comfortable shoes!

Hire a pro or go it alone, but don't just sit there, y'all—get out there and explore! ❁

That's how we roll: Whether it's from the driver's seat of an **Old Savannah Tours** trolley *(see ad to right)* or while pedaling a three-wheeled pedicab, Savannah's many tour guides each have a unique take on three hundred years of history.

Savannah's Stars
By Laura Clark

In a city where the past echoes through the present like the sounds of horses' hooves through brick-paved streets, the legacies of Savannah's most accomplished sons and daughters are celebrated on a daily basis. Check out these national notables who once called Savannah home.

Charles Coburn. *(1877-1961)* With an Academy Award®, over 40 movie roles and a star on the Hollywood Walk of Fame to his name, Coburn was an actor much beloved for his comedic roles and smooth, low voice.

Clarence Thomas. *(1948-)* Born just outside of Savannah in the small settlement of Pinpoint, Georgia, Justice Thomas was appointed a U.S. Supreme Court Judge in 1991—becoming the second African-American to take a seat on the country's highest court.

Conrad Aiken. *(1889-1973)* Born in a house near Savannah's **Colonial Park Cemetery**, the poet spent much of his childhood in Massachusetts after the murder-suicide of his father and mother. Following a successful writing career that had him named Poetry Consultant to the Library of Congress, Aiken returned to his beloved Hostess City. He is buried at **Bonaventure Cemetery** under a bench engraved with the intriguingly poetic epilogue "Cosmos Mariner, Destination Unknown."

Flannery O'Connor. *(1925-1964)* A writer of the dark but humorous Southern Gothic genre, O'Connor spent the first formative years of her life at 207 East Charlton Street. Today, the modest home in the shadow of the **Cathedral of St. John the Baptist** is open to the public as a museum dedicated to the author's early life. Visitors can even enjoy a bit of shade in the very backyard where O'Connor is known to have trained a chicken to walk backwards.

Johnny Mercer. *(1909-1976)* Arguably the most famous and beloved of all Savannahians, the prolific singer/songwriter and co-founder of Capitol Records penned some of America's favorite songs, including "Come Rain or Come Shine," "Skylark," "Jeepers Creepers," "You Must Have Been a Beautiful Baby," and "Moon River." Mercer's talent earned him four Academy Awards® and a bronze statue in **Ellis Square**. *(opposite)*

© Chia Chong Photography

© Juliette Gordon Low Birthplace

Juliette Gordon Low. *(1860-1927)* The founder of the Girl Scouts of the U.S.A., "Daisy," as she was known to family and friends, spent most of her life in Savannah and used the city as a home base for her burgeoning organization. Today, there are two historic sites in the city involving the philanthropist and female empowerment activist: **The Juliette Gordon Low Birthplace** at 10 East Oglethorpe and the **Girl Scout's First Headquarters** at 330 Drayton Street. *(left)*

Paula Deen. *(1947-)* Iconic restaurateur, cookbook author and *Food Network* star got her start on the southside of Savannah making box lunches for office folks. Famous for her love of real Southern cooking and unapologetic use of butter, Paula films many of her shows at her residence on Wilmington Island, where she lives with her boat captain husband, Michael Groover. *(above)*

Ruby Gettinger. *(1975-)* Charming and compassionate, Ruby's self-titled *Style Network* reality show has become a runaway hit its past two seasons. Folks from all over the world have fallen in love with this redhead working to reach a healthy weight with humor and honesty while providing indefatigable inspiration to all.

Uga VIII. *(2010-)* One of Savannah's most famous residents spends most of his life in the doghouse. The University of Georgia's cherished mascot comes from a cherished bloodline kept and cared for by local celebrity and lawyer Frank "Sonny" Seiler, who personally delivers the bulldog to every UGA home game.

© Bryan Stovall

© Bryan S

Above the Door and Behind the Curtains

AN ARCHITECTURAL TOUR OF SAVANNAH'S HISTORIC HOMES

By Allison Hersh

In this perfectly preserved city, it's possible to traverse several centuries in a few square blocks. Start at the Savannah River and walk south on any major street downtown to observe a chronological progression of architectural styles, from stately federal brick to lacy Victorian touches. While most homes are still privately owned, visitors are welcome at many of these grand residences.

The **Isaiah Davenport House** on Columbia Square was originally built in 1820 and has been meticulously restored to its original grandeur after being saved from demolition by a group of seven dedicated local women who formed the core of the Historic Savannah Foundation. This Federal-style brick home is now a museum where docents in period dress interpret the life of an early 19th-century Savannah family. (*324 E. State Street, 912.236.8097, davenporthousemuseum.org*)

Two homes associated with one famous Savannah resident are open to visitors: The **Juliette Gordon Low Birthplace** was built by Savannah mayor and U.S. Supreme Court Justice James M. Wayne in 1818, but it earned its place in history when a young woman known as "Daisy" started the Girl Scouts of the USA in the back parlor in 1912. (*10 E. Oglethorpe Avenue, 912.233.4501, juliettegordonlowbirthplace.org*)

Juliette's home in adulthood, the **Andrew Low House** on Lafayette Square, is packed with antique furniture and other items used by this wealthy Savannah family. Visitors will follow in the footsteps of General Robert E. Lee, who was a frequent guest in the home. Both homes are popular stops for Girl Scout troops visiting Savannah. (*329 Abercorn Street, 912.233.6854, andrewlowhouse.com*)

© Bryan Stovall *© Bryan Stovall*

Elegance reigns supreme at the **Owens-Thomas House**, widely considered the finest example of English Regency architecture in America. Designed by British architect William Jay, this National Historic Landmark overlooking Oglethorpe Square is one of the **Telfair Museum's** landmark buildings in Savannah. The home's collection of neoclassical furnishings, English-inspired parterre garden and original carriage house—which contains one of the earliest intact urban slave quarters in the South—attract visitors from around the world. *(124 Abercorn Street, 912.233.9743, telfair.org)*

A breath-taking double entrance, the parapet with its swooping elliptical arches and Doric columns on the portico make the **Sorrel-Weed House** one of the finest examples of antebellum Greek Revival/Regency architecture in the country. Restored to its former glory right down to the original orange paint, this National Historic Trust Landmark is also well-known as one of the most haunted destinations in Savannah. *(6 W. Harris Street, 912.236.8888, sorrelweedhouse.com)*

Overlooking Lafayette Square, the **Flannery O'Connor Childhood Home** is dedicated to preserving the legacy of one of the South's greatest writers. This 1856 home has been meticulously restored to reflect the authentic period furnishings of a Depression-era rowhouse and to offer insight into the years that O'Connor lived in Savannah, from 1925 to 1938. This historic home features many items from the writer's childhood, including her monogrammed baby carriage and an extensive library once owned by her family. *(207 E. Charlton Street, 912.233.6014, flanneryoconnorhome.org)*

The **Green-Meldrim House** overlooking Madison Square stands apart as one of the finest examples of Gothic Revival architecture in the United States. Located adjacent to St. John's Episcopal Church, which operates the mansion as its parish house, this

Opposite left: The past lives on at the **Isaiah Davenport House**. *Opposite right:* The **Juliette Gordon Low Birthplace** hosts legions of Girl Scouts throughout the year. *Above left:* Girl Scouts also flock to the **Andrew Low House**, Juliette's home in adulthood. *(see ad - page 44) Above right:* The **Green-Meldrim** is one of the finest examples of Gothic Revival architecture in the country.

stunning house served as Union General William T. Sherman's posh headquarters during the Civil War in December 1864. In fact, he wrote his famous telegram that presented Savannah to President Abraham Lincoln as a Christmas present from a bedroom at this luxurious home. Unusual arched windows, sandstone parapet edging and intricate wrought iron detailing give this home, built for cotton merchant Charles Green in 1850, a distinctive neo-Gothic style. *(14 W. Macon Street, 912.233.3845, stjohnssav.org)*

The **Mercer House** plays a major role in John Berendt's bestseller, *Midnight in the Garden of Good and Evil*, serving as the home of antiques dealer and preservationist Jim Williams, whose murder serves as a central event in "The Book." Designed in 1860 for Hugh W. Mercer (the great-grandfather of Academy Award®-winning songwriter Johnny Mercer,) this brick mansion anchors Monterey Square and is open for tours. The home showcases an extensive collection of rare antiques, while the carriage house overlooking Whitaker Street is home to a popular local gift shop. *(429 Bull Street, 912.238.0208, mercerhouse.com)*

For a comprehensive look at the city's African-American history, don't miss the **King-Tisdell Cottage**, a restored Victorian structure that now serves as an African-American heritage museum. Built in 1896, this cottage houses exhibits focusing upon Savannah and the neighboring sea islands steeped in Gullah-Geechee culture. Highlights at the museum include rare artifacts, including a bill of sale for slaves written in Arabic. *(514 E. Huntingdon Street, 912.234.8000, kingtisdell.org)*

Magnolia Hall, which serves as a private guest house for the Savannah College of Art and Design, features three stories of Victorian charm overlooking Forsyth Park. This elegant three-story residence boasts a sloping mansard roof façade with decorative ornamental brackets and deep, double-tiered verandas. Originally built in 1878 for cotton magnate Jacob Guerard Heyward and operated as a historic inn for many years, Magnolia Hall also served as the birthplace of Pulitzer Prize-winning poet and novelist Conrad Aiken. *(507 Whitaker Street, 912.525.5000, scad.edu)*

Nestled in the heart of Savannah's Thomas Square Streetcar Historic District, **The Gingerbread House** stands apart as one of the country's finest examples of Steamboat Gothic architecture. Formerly known as the Asendorf House, this architectural treasure was originally built in 1899 and now hosts a number of weddings and private parties throughout the year. With elaborate gingerbread arches and decorative spindles, this house has a Victorian charm that appeals to visitors from near and far. *(1921 Bull Street, 912.234.7303)*

About 15 miles from downtown towards Isle of Hope lies the 18th-century remains of **Wormsloe Plantation**. Built in 1733 by founding Georgia colonist Noble Jones, the site offers visitors a chance to explore a museum full of artifacts, the tabby ruins of the fort and nature trails through the maritime forest. Check the web site for "living history" events throughout the year (closed Mondays.) The breathtaking entrance through 1.5-mile canopy of live oaks is worth the trip alone! *(7601 Skidaway Road, 912.353.3023, gastateparks. org/info/wormsloe)* ❈

Top: The **Owens-Thomas House** is a fine example of English Regency architecture and a popular stop for visitors. *(see ad - page 98)* Middle: All your fairytale wedding dreams can come true at the Victorian-inspired **Gingerbread House**. Bottom: Experience the majestic oak canopy at **Wormsloe Plantation**.

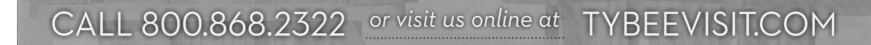

A Day at the Beach

"Savannah's Beach" offers sun, sand and so much more

By Jessica Leigh Lebos

© Bryan Stovall

Less than a half hour's leisurely drive from the sophisticated bustle of Savannah's downtown district, there's a quirky little beach town with a personality all its own. The dress code: Flip flops. The attitude: Laidback. The agenda: Whatever you like.

With five miles of uninterrupted beach spread out between the mouth of the Savannah River and the Atlantic Ocean, Tybee is the northernmost link in the chain of barrier islands known as Georgia's "Golden Isles." If it feels like a world away, it should: The island is separated from the mainland by one of the largest expanses of saltwater marsh on the East coast. The name *Tybee* is derived from a word meaning "salt" in the language of the Euchee, a native tribe of hunters and fishermen who seasonably migrated from the mainland a millennia ago.

While a favorite haunt of 18th-century pirates—local lore claims that Blackbeard's treasure is buried on one of the islands just south—the island didn't become a resort destination until 1887, when the small community of "Ocean City" opened its first hotels and rental cottages to accommodate Savannah's wealthy. The trip was made from downtown in three hours by steamship or two hours by train, but in 1923, a palm-lined highway replaced the tracks and opened up the island to anyone with car and full tank of gas.

Since then, Tybee has fulfilled the getaway fantasies of folks from all over the world. Plenty of hotels, motels, spacious vacation homes with wraparound porches, charming rental cottages in rainbow colors and a full-service campground mean every budget can accommodate a beach vacation. Those who like to wile away the day with a cold one in hand watching the ships pass by need only a chair and a tube of sunscreen. Folks with a little more ambition can spend the day browsing the beachwear shops on **Tybrisa Street** or the artists' collectives at **Tybee Oaks**, exploring estuaries and wildlife in a kayak, harnessing the wind on a kiteboard or simply strolling the beach looking for sharks' teeth.

Voted "Healthiest Beach" by *Health* magazine in 2009, Tybee hosts an annual marathon, international bicycle races, national sailing and speed boat races, kayak races, surfing, kiteboarding and other competitions that attract athletes, weekend warriors and legions of spectators. But you don't need to be a contender to enjoy an active lifestyle where it's okay to relax at the same time (even

© Bryan Stovall

Opposite: The view goes both ways on the **Tybee Pier and Pavilion**.

Left: You can see for miles and miles from the top of the historic **Tybee Lighthouse**.

the rental bikes have cupholders to accommodate a beverage.) The flat island even has its own version of a hike with a view: Climbing the 178 steps to the top of the historic **Tybee Lighthouse**.

One thing you must know about Tybee is that for most every major occasion, there's a parade. Tybee Island is famous for its annual wet and wild Beach Bum Parade Memorial Day Weekend, an Irish Heritage Parade near St. Patrick's Day full of gold coin-throwing leprechauns, a Mardi Gras procession with enough beads to rival New Orleans, and the family-friendly Pirate Festival parade in the fall to honor the island's first and heartiest partyers. No one lets the weather rain on any parades here either: Santa Claus cruises down Butler Avenue every December, and the New Year's Day Polar Bear Plunge is a processional that leads right into January's chilly Atlantic. Throughout the year you might care to plan your trip around the sand castle competitions, a vintage car show, arts and craft fairs, a wine festival and the not-to-be-missed Independence Day pyrotechnic extravaganza, usually held July 3.

Planning a wedding? **Romantic Weddings of Savannah** can help you tie the knot on Tybee Island any day of the week on the beach—or you and your beloved can walk down the aisle at

the **Tybee Island Wedding Chapel**, the church built by Disney Studios for the Miley Cyrus movie "The Last Song," filmed on location here in 2009. If you and your beloved enjoy a crowd, you can participate in the country's largest "group wedding and vow renewal" ceremony, held every on Valentine's Day. Restaurants abound to host rehearsal dinners and receptions, and of course, the beach is a honeymoon destination like none other!

But be assured: it all comes back to the sand, the sea and the beauty here. In spite of thousands of visitors, this is still a place where pod of dolphins or a particularly stunning sunset on the Back River can stop what little traffic there is. The pelicans still outnumber the permanent residents, and the sea turtles are honored citizens. As much as there is to do on Tybee Island, don't forget to let yourself drift into what locals call "Tybee Time," that quiet, happy dimension where the best place to be is exactly where you are. ❀

For complete information on Tybee Island's attractions, festivals and activities, go to *www.tybeevisit.com.* (see ad - page 61)

Take It Outside

By Laura Clark

From golf course greens to untouched sands, the great outdoors has something for everyone.

Enveloped within its romantic squares and shaded streets, it is easy to forget that a world exists beyond Savannah's historic downtown. It has a transcendent power, as though a sultry island in time. Yet to fail to see beyond Savannah's urban majesty is to ignore the many rustic treasures that make the city a haven for nature-loving excursionists. Mere miles from the warm waters of the Atlantic Ocean and intertwined by snaking rivers and expansive marsh lands, the Savannah area's unique natural positioning provides visitors with enough outdoor options to keep even the most ambitious eco-tourist satisfied. Whether a tried and true outdoorsman, or a homebody just looking for some pretty views and a touch of a tan, we've got something for everyone.

Hit the Greens

It only makes sense that golf is a big game in a place so full of natural beauty and continual sunshine. Despite the fact that we are a drive away from Augusta and its famous greens, Savannah has made its own name for itself among the national golf community thanks to a collection of pristine private courses and owners committed to evolving excellence. Club-toting visitors can head over the Talmadge Bridge to Hutchinson Island to tee off at **The Club at Savannah Harbor,** a ball's toss from the entrance to the **Westin Savannah Harbor Golf Resort & Spa**. Situated on an island preserve, the 18-hole PGA championship golf course was designed by Robert Cupp and

Sam Snead and offers excitement for both novice and experienced players. Annual tournaments like the Liberty Legends of Golf regularly bring new players to the area, but you don't have to be a pro to enjoy 18 holes.

Other stunning area greens include **Crosswinds Golf Club** (conveniently located near Savannah-Hilton Head International Airport), **Henderson Golf Club** (on the marsh near Highways 204 and 17), Rees Jones-designed **Southbridge Golf Club** (off I-16) and **Bacon Park Golf Course**, the city's public course on the south side of town.

Fishing Fun

The waters of the Lowcountry are teaming with marine life ensuring that anglers of any skill set will find excitement. Casting a reel in the peaceful back rivers might catch you spotted sea bass, flounder or tarpon, depending upon the season. For bigger game, including mahi-mahi, tuna, bluefish and barracuda, head out to the Gulf Stream or to one of Georgia's artificial reefs.

"There is just so much to see here," explains Captain Judy Helmey, owner of **Miss Judy Charters**, a favorite among a growing collection of Savannah-area charter companies aimed at providing visitors with unforgettable oceanic experiences. According to Captain Judy, the exquisite natural settings make fishing in the area particularly special. "We turn our fishing trips into an experience. I love taking people who have never been and showing them the sea life and wildlife we have here."

Offering off-shore and in-shore charters as well as specialty trips (including shark fishing excursions), Captain Judy mixes expertise with over 50 years of passion for the local environment, making each trip out a unique journey. Visitors seeking more information on what to expect below the blue should check out Captain Judy's fishing reports posted weekly on her website, *missjudycharters.com*.

Paddle Party

In Savannah, there's more than one way to hit the water, as the area's thriving kayak and canoeing community will be sure to tell you. Where narrow marshland waterways lead to hidden natural treasures, and where rare birds nest while dolphins play in the shallow water, a paddle, a vessel and a knowledgeable guide is all you need for an unforgettable day.

"Georgia has the largest expanse of salt marsh of any coastal state," says Nigel Law, co-owner of **Savannah Canoe and Kayak** (*savannahcanoeandkayak.com*), which offers canoeing and kayaking instruction, guided tours, and camping adventures. "The marsh is such a vibrant green in the summer months, but its overall character is one of peace and tranquility. It is a very calming environment and the kayak slips through the maze of tidal creeks barely noticed. We quickly become a part of that tranquility."

Also smitten with the coastal charm is Rebecca Parris, co-owner of **North Island Surf and Kayak** (*northislandkayak.com*) on Tybee Island. Offering tours, lessons and kayak rental, the company's excursions are intended to awe and inspire. "We want visitors to have a memorable vacation and to really enjoy themselves," she says. "But we also stress an appreciation for the environment and how important it is to respect and to nurture it."

Park It

For city-bound nature-lovers looking for a grassy respite, the historic (and historically beautiful) Forsyth Park offers everything from playing fields and picturesque walking paths to flower gardens and shaded benches. A 30-acre green space in the middle of historic downtown Savannah, **Forsyth Park** was originally established in the 1840s and once hosted some of Sherman's troops during the Union occupation of Savannah in the Civil War.

Today, instead of foxholes dotting the huge lawns on the park's east and west sides, you'll see sunbathers, picnicking families and athletes playing every sport from football to lacrosse. Take a brisk walk around the park's perimeter to admire the elegant surrounding facades of Savannah's Victorian District and don't forget to head down to the south end to check out the famed Forsyth Park

Opposite: Tee off under the **Talmadge Bridge** on the courses at the **Club at Savannah Harbor**. *Above:* Even a bad day fishing is still pretty good, especially when surrounded by pristine coastal marshes.

Fountain, which recently celebrated over 150 years as the city's favorite photo-op. Beyond the fountain, you'll find two playgrounds for the kids as well as the brand new **Forsyth Park Visitor Center** inside the old fort, housing a restaurant and bar as well as an outdoor stage for concerts.

Wild Out

Animal lovers and amateur naturalists looking for nothing less than a wild experience should inquire into the regular tours and excursions led by **Wilderness Southeast** (*wilderness-southeast.org*), a non-profit educational organization leading nature enthusiasts into the untamed side of coastal Georgia since 1973.

Private tours suited to personal interests or needs are available, but group expeditions are also offered. Accompanied by educated and enthusiastic guides, you could troll marshland for alligators and anhingas, go bird watching, visit river swamps to spy on reptiles or take a forest walk to learn about useful native plants. The tours are both informational and fun—it doesn't get much better than that.

Beach Bumming

Where there's a beach, there has to be fun, and this holds especially true on Tybee Island, Savannah's coastal neighbor. Sure, you could spend the day lounging on Tybee's white-sanded tidal shores, but why work on a tan when you could be indulging in any number of beachside extreme sports including surfing, kiteboarding and stand-up paddle boarding.

No gear? Not even sure what stand-up paddle boarding is? Worry not—the island is home to several shops offering equipment rental and instruction. The people at **High Tide Surf Shop** (*hightidesurfshop.com*) spend their days enlightening visitors to Tybee's favorite seaside sports.

"We pioneered kite surfing lessons on the island 10 years ago with a safe and easy instruction technique, but right now requests for [stand-up] paddle boarding lessons are just exploding," explains manager Tim Malins, who highly recommends the relatively new sport that could be described as a mix between surfing and canoeing. "It's easy to learn and offers very quick gratification. There isn't much frustration to have fun."

Pedal Pushers

There is perhaps no better way to enjoy a breezy tour of the area than at the pedals of a bike. Savannah's flat landscape and street-side sights make it an ideal biking city and the same goes for the near-by Tybee Island, where ocean views and cultural locales including the historic lighthouse makes biking a special treat.

Formal bike tours are available on the mainland, but for the adventurous looking to lead their own way, seek out rental opportunities at a local shop. In Savannah, stop into **Bicycle Link** (*bicyclelinksav.com*), and **Fat Tire Bikes** (*fattirebikestybee.com*) will suit your needs on Tybee.

Looking for something a little more adventurous than a city tour? The area has several alluring parks and refuges to challenge you. Check out the **Savannah National Wildlife Refuge** (*fws.gov/savannah*) for moderately-rugged terrain and a promise to see a variety of flora and fauna, including the Lowcountry's ubiquitous alligators. ❁

Top: The classic fountain at the center of **Forsyth Park** serves as a sublime sitting spot for all ages. *Bottom:* Explore the open ocean on a charter fishing vessel.

Hollywood Heads South

Savannah has long lent her beauty to movie producers in search of the perfect filming location for their next blockbuster as well as national television commercials and magazine layouts. Today, in the wake of over 60 film crews, a stroll through Savannah is like a walk behind the scenes of one of America's most elegant movie sets—if you know where to look. Keep an eye out for familiar Lowcountry locales in these feature films:

Cape Fear *(1962)* Starring Gregory Peck, Robert Mitchum and Polly Bergen, this classic crime thriller filmed at several Savannah locales including Armstrong House at 447 Bull Street.

The Longest Yard *(1974)* Before ending up in prison and coaching a football team of misfits, Burt Reynolds leads police on a tire-squealing chase through Forsyth Park and around its picturesque fountain.

Gator *(1976)* Burt Reynolds returned to Savannah to direct and star as a moonshine-making ex-con in this sequel to *White Lightning*.

Glory *(1989)* The story of the Civil War's first black volunteer company, this three-time Oscar® winner emptied Monterey Square of its hanging moss to make the locale appear as part of a New England City.

Camilla *(1993)* Filmed downtown and at Fort Pulaski on U. S. Highway 80, this independently-produced road trip saga starred Jessica Tandy and Bridget Fonda.

Forrest Gump *(1994)* A winner of six Oscars®, the producers of this timeless tearjerker built a bench on the north end of Chippewa Square (where a flowerbed now sits) as the memorable setting for Tom Hanks' famous character.

Now and Then *(1995)* This coming-of-age story set in 1970 in a small town was filmed in Savannah and Statesboro, Georgia.

Something to Talk About *(1995)* Starring Julia Roberts and Dennis Quaid, a pivotal scene of this blockbuster was filmed in the atmospheric Johnson Square.

Midnight in the Garden of Good and Evil *(1997)* As the Hollywood adaptation of John Berendt's bestselling book about a Savannah murder trial, this movie filmed throughout the Historic District.

The Gingerbread Man *(1997)* John Grisham's noir-ish screenplay about an embattled Savannah attorney trying to help a mysterious woman found a perfect setting among the moss curtains and sultry atmosphere.

The General's Daughter *(1998)* This military mystery starring John Travolta filmed a scene at the historic Wormsloe Plantation, where the oak-lined drive lent the movie an extra level of drama.

Forces of Nature *(1999)* Romantic comedy veterans Sandra Bullock and Ben Affleck trade barbs and laughs under a giant globe that can be viewed heading south on Abercorn.

The Legend of Bagger Vance *(2000)* Starring Will Smith, Matt Damon and Charlize Theron, this Robert Redford-directed homage to the game of golf is set in 1920s Savannah and was filmed on its streets and surrounding countryside.

The Gift *(2000)* Set in the fictional southern town of Brixton, Georgia, and filmed in multiple locales throughout the Peach State, this horror movie starred Cate Blanchett, Keanu Reeves and Katie Holmes.

The Haunted Mansion *(2003)* Perhaps Savannah's reputation for ghosts attracted Disney Studios to film segments of this Eddie Murphy comedy based on the wildly-popular theme park attraction.

The Last Song *(2010)* This dramatic father-daughter tale starring Miley Cyrus and Greg Kinnear was filmed outside of Savannah on nearby Tybee Island throughout summer 2009.

The Conspirator *(2010)* Robert Redford returned to the streets of Savannah to shoot this film about the aftermath of the assassination of Abraham Lincoln, starring Justin Long, Evan Rachel Wood and Robin Wright Penn.

© Bryan Stovall

© Kevin Nightingale

Final Resting Places

By Jessica Leigh Lebos

Their residents may be six feet under, but above ground, Savannah's historic cemeteries boast some of the most compelling scenery in the nation. Notable historical figures, war heroes and the occasional ghost can be sought among hand-cut grave markers and luxuriant foliage, giving visitors plenty of reason to commune with Savannah's dead and buried.

Within walking distance of other downtown sites is **Colonial Park**, stretching across six acres and accessed through a tall gate at the corner of Oglethorpe and Abercorn Streets. The city interred its prominent citizens here from 1750 to 1853—steamship magnate William Scarborough has a marker here, as does Button Gwinnet, one of the signers of the Declaration of Independence—though the majority of the graves are unmarked. Many rich symbols are inscribed in the headstones; many feature trees whose height represents the length of the deceased's life. Also be on the lookout for poppies (symbolizing death's long sleep,) overturned hourglasses and ominous-looking scythes. It's also a favorite stop on ghost tours.

Savannah's most famous final resting place is **Bonaventure Cemetery**, occupying a scenic spot on the Wilmington River just east of town. Created in the mid-1800s on the site of a former plantation by the same name, many visitors come to Bonaventure because of its association with the best-selling novel, *Midnight in the Garden of Good and Evil* by John Berendt. Photographer Jack Leigh's iconic image on the cover of *Midnight* features a statue known as the Bird Girl, which used to stand over the Bonaventure grave of Lucy Boyd Trosdal but has been moved to the Telfair Museum of Art in downtown Savannah. Famous residents include Revolutionary War patriot Noble Wimberly Jones, crooner Johnny Mercer and poet Conrad Aiken.

Established by the city as an annex to the Bonaventure grounds in 1933, **Greenwich Cemetery** is worth a visit to experience its tranquil gardens and river bluff views. Full of ancient statuary and exotic plant life, these 65 acres were once home to one of the most majestic privately-held estates in the South, of which an elegant white marble fountain, a few outbuildings and a small pond remain as reminders of the past.

Laurel Grove Cemetery North and **Laurel Grove Cemetery South** don't get nearly the amount of visitors as Bonaventure, and these sprawling 150,000 acres on the western edge of the city provide a far-reaching serenity. As you traverse the grounds, be on the lookout for the huge Gettysburg section, with over 700 Confederate burials from the Civil War, and "Baby Land," a collection of tiny statues dedicated to Laurel Grove's youngest residents.

Split into northern and southern sections in the 1800s, white Savannahians were traditionally buried in Laurel Grove North and black Savannahians in Laurel Grove South. At least 24 Savannah mayors rest in the north section, alongside nine Civil War Generals, one U.S. Supreme Court Justice, Girl Scouts of America founder Juliette Gordon Low, "Waving Girl" Francis Martus and "Jingle Bells" composer James Pierpont. Established in 1853 as a dedicated burial place for slaves and "free persons of color," the south section provides eternal rest to many of Savannah's prominent African-American leaders, including First African Baptist minister Andrew Bryan. A major revitalization took place of Laurel Grove South in the 1970s, led by civil rights activist W. W. Law.

Privately owned and maintained by the Catholic Diocese of Savannah, the **Catholic Cemetery** tucked away past Skidaway Road on Wheaton Street. Bucolic and off the beaten path, these oak-filled acres contain the remains of many of Savannah's Irish citizens, including members of the Confederate Army's Jasper Greens. Still active, it serves as an important site to city's strong Irish heritage and history.

Situated on a forgotten strip of land near two freeways off West Boundary Street, the **Old Jewish Burial Ground** stands behind tall concrete walls. Established in 1733 by Mordecai Sheftall from the land granted to him by King George II of England, the small cemetery contains the graves of the some of the earliest founders of Mickve Israel, the third-oldest Jewish congregation in the country. ❀

© Bryan Stovall

Opposite left: **Colonial Park Cemetary** happens to be one of the prettiest parks in town. *Opposite right:* Angels among the grave stones at **Bonaventure Cemetery**. *Left:* **Laurel Grove Cemetary** is the city's largest and likely most peaceful.

explore | directory

Andrew Low House | *p. 44*

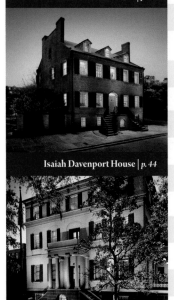

Isaiah Davenport House | *p. 44*

Juliette Gordon Low Birthplace | *p. 44*

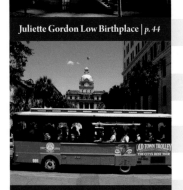

Old Town Trolley | *p. 25, 53, 69*

Andrew Low House	**912.233.6854**	**329 Abercorn Street**	**andrewlowhouse.com**
Bacon Park Golf Course	912.354.2625	1 Shorty Cooper Drive	baconparkgolf.com
City Market	**912.232.4903**	**219 W. Bryan Street, Suite 207**	**savannahcitymarket.com**
The Club at Savannah Harbor	912.201.2240	#2 Resort Drive	theclubatsavannahharbor.com
Coastal Heritage Society	**912.651.6840**	**303 MLK Jr. Boulevard**	**chsgeorgia.org**
Crosswinds Golf Club	912.966.1909	232 James B. Blackburn Drive	crosswindsgolfclub.com
Flannery O'Connor Childhood Home	912.233.6014	207 E. Charlton Street	flanneryoconnorhome.org
Garden City CVB	912.963.2750	100 Central Ave. *(Garden City)*	gardencityga.org
The Gingerbread House	912.239.9652	1921 Bull Street	
Green-Meldrim House	912.233.3845	14 W. Macon Street	
Henderson Golf Club	912.920.4653	1 Al Henderson Drive	hendersongolfclub.com
Historic Savannah Carriage Tours	912.443.9333	100 Aberdeen Street	savannahcarriage.com
Historic Savannah Foundation	912.233.7787	321 E. York Street	myhsf.org
Isaiah Davenport House	**912.236.8097**	**324 E. State Street**	**davenporthousemuseum.org**
Juliette Gordon Low Birthplace	**912.233.4502**	**10 E. Oglethorpe Avenue**	**juliettegordonlowbirthplace.org**
Kelly Tours, Inc.	843.681.9911	5 Hawk Court	kellytours.com
Keytosavannah.com	912.356.1140		keytosavannah.com
King Tisdell Cottage	912.234.8000	514 E. Huntingdon Street	kingtisdell.org
Liberty Mutual Legends of Golf	912.236.1333	101 E. Bay Street	lmlog.com
Magnolia Hall	912.525.5000	507 Whitaker Street	
Mercer House	912.236.6352	430 Whitaker Street	mercerhouse.com
Oglethorpe Tours	912.233.8380	7 Rathborne Road	oglethorpetours.com
Old Savannah Tours	**912.234.8128**	**250 MLK Jr. Boulevard**	**oldsavannahtours.com**
Old Town Trolley Tours	**912.233.0083**	**234 MLK Jr. Boulevard**	**trolleytours.com/savannah**

Owens-Thomas House	**912.233.9743**	**124 Abercorn Street**	**telfair.org**
Plantation Carriage Co.	912.236.4331	219 W. Bryan Street, Suite 303	
Romantic Weddings of Savannah	912.856.2165		romanticweddingsofsavannah.com
River Street Market Place	912.495.0014	502 E. River Street	riverstreetmarketplace.com
River Street Riverboat Company	**912.232.6404**	**9 E. River Street**	**savannahriverboat.com**
Savannah Fun Tours	912.667.9760	206 E. Taylor Street	savannahfuntours.com
Savannah/Hilton Head International Airport	**912.964.0514**	**400 Airways Avenue**	**savannahairport.com**
Savannah International Trade and Convention Center	912.447.4000	One International Drive	savtcc.com
Savannah SandGnats	**912.351.9150**	**1401 E. Victory Drive**	**sandgnats.com**
Savannah Riverfront	**912.234.0295**	**404 E. Bay Street**	**riverstreetsavannah.com**
The Savannah Walks Inc.	912.238.9255	37 Abercorn Street	savannahwalks.com
Segway of Savannah	912.233.3554	102 E. Liberty Street, Suite 106	segwayofsavannah.com
Shannon Vineyards	912.660.5582	4197 Savannah Highway *(Sylvania)*	shannonvineyards.com
Sixth Sense Savannah Ghost Tours	912.292.0960	1 Stauffer Court	sixthsensesavannah.com
Sorrel-Weed House	912.236.8888	6 W. Harris Street	sorrelweedhouse.com
Southbridge Golf Club	912.651.5455	415 Southbridge Boulevard	southbridgegolfclub.com
Swept Away Trailways/ Gray Line Savannah	912.236.9604 x101	1115 Louisville Road	sweptawaytours.com
Telfair Academy	**912.790.8800**	**121 Barnard Street**	**telfair.org**
Tybee Island Marine Science Center	**912.272.5008**	**1510 Strand Street**	**tybeemarinescience.org**
Tybee Island Wedding Chapel	**888.988.9233**	**1112 US Highway 80**	**tybeeweddingchapel.com**
Tybee Lighthouse	912.786.5801	30 Meddin Avenue	tybeelighthouse.org
Tybee Tourism Council	**800.868.2322**		**tybeevisit.com**
University of South Carolina Beaufort	843.208.8218	1 University Boulevard *(Bluffton, SC)*	uscb.edu
Visit Savannah	**877.SAVANNAH**	**301 MLK Jr. Boulevard**	**visitsavannah.com**
Wormsloe Plantation	912.353.3023	7601 Skidaway Road	gastateparks.org/wormsloe

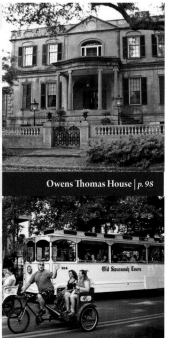

Owens Thomas House | *p. 98*

Old Savannah Tours | *p. 55*

Tybee Marine Science Center | *p. 63*

River Street Riverboat Company | *p. 54*

SAVANNAH MUSIC FESTIVAL

MARCH 24 - APRIL 9, 2011
MARCH 22 - APRIL 7, 2012

"What other festival allows you to start the evening with a string quartet and finish it by listening to bluegrass over a beer?"
–Financial Times (UK)

JAZZ CLASSICAL AMERICANA WORLD MUSIC

For Tickets: www.savannahmusicfestival.org or (912) 525-5050

The Historic Savannah Theatre has been delighting audiences for 10 years with sensational fast-paced, family-friendly musical shows — perfect for a Southern evening's fun! Rock and roll, pop, country, jazz and Broadway are combined with side-splittting comedy and performed by professional singers, dancers and live band on stage year-round in America's oldest operating theatre. Don't miss it!

In our 10th Year as Savannah's #1 Entertainment!

The Savannah Theatre

Mention This Ad For Special Savings!

Saturday and Sunday Matinees @ 3pm
Wednesday through Saturday and select Tuesdays @ 8pm

222 Bull Street at Chippewa Square in Historic Downtown Savannah, GA

Get your tickets today! 912-233-7764 or www.savannahtheatre.com

Children experiencing Old Fort Jackson

experience|*savannah*

amusement for all ages | higher education | what to do after dark | just relax | an eternal romance | art around every corner | homage to history

It could be the way light is captured on canvas as it dapples through moss-draped oaks. Or maybe it's the urban grit of an underground spoken word scene. Perhaps locomotives and cannon firings are what make your eyes go wide—whatever your preferred aesthetic, there's something to spark your passion in Savannah. Fine art and architecture enthusiasts already know they'll be kept busy by our famous historic homes, monument-studded squares and the oldest public art museum in the South. But this sophisticated port city also presents an astonishing array of modern art exhibits, outdoor sculptures, cutting-edge architecture and unique children's activities as well as thriving film and theater communities. Add in hundreds of working artists and photographers and one of the most respected design schools in the country, and the result is a dynamic buzz of history-meets-hip all year long.

© Bryan Stovall

© Telfair Museum of Art

Amusement for All Ages

IN SAVANNAH, THERE'S NEVER A REASON TO HEAR "I'M BORED" FROM PINT-SIZE MEMBERS OF YOUR TRAVELING PARTY.
HERE'S A CHECKLIST OF THINGS TO WITH THE KIDS—OR WITHOUT!

By Jessica Leigh Lebos

Ride a Locomotive

601 W. Harris Street | 912.651.6823 | chsgeorgia.org

Thomas the Tank Engine would have felt right at home at **The Roundhouse Railroad Museum**, where a giant turntable still shifts cars onto tracks. Little engineers can learn about the history of steam engines and belt-driven machinery, and model train buffs will kick up their heels at the huge display of downtown Savannah! The museum is open daily, but train rides are seasonal—call ahead to check the schedule. Families will find even more to do at this historical complex run by the Coastal Heritage Society, including exploration of **Battlefield Park** and lunch at the **WhistleStop Café**.

Be an Architect

207 W. York Street Savannah | 912.790.8800 | telfair.org

You can build a likeness of one of Savannah's historic homes or create something no one's ever seen before with the blocks at **ArtZeum at Telfair Museum's Jepson Center for the Arts**. The two-level, 3500 square-foot gallery has plenty more to keep those little hands busy, including a magnetic sculpture wall and other interactive exhibits using works from the Telfair collection.

© Erin Adams Photography

Dine with Pirates

20 East Broad Street | 912.233.5757 | thepirateshouse.com

Legend has it that Captain Flint from the Robert Louis Stevenson classic "Treasure Island" died in an upstairs room at what is now **The Pirates' House Restaurant** with first mate, Billy Bones, at his side. This landmark eatery opened in 1753 as an inn for seafarers—you can still explore the tunnel where unsuspecting sailors were shanghaied onto pirate ships. Keep your eyes open for pirates in the dining room ready to pose for photos between courses!

Cozy Up with a Wolf

711 Sandtown Road | 912.395.1212 | oatlandisland.org

Just minutes from downtown, the Wolf Wilderness habitat at **Oatland Island Wildlife Center** gives folks nose-to-nose access with a pack of gray wolves (with a thick Plexiglass window in between, of course.) The air-conditioned wolf observation cabin is part of an easy two-mile nature trail that winds through lush Lowcountry forest and serene marsh past bison, panthers, owls, eagles, farm animals and other local flora and fauna.

© Tybee Island Marine Science Center

Touch a Sand Dollar

1510 Strand Avenue, Tybee Island | 912.786.5917 | tybeemarinescience.org

Depending on the day, the touch tank at the **Tybee Island Marine Science Center** is swimming with creatures native to the Georgia Coast, including whelk, hermit crabs, starfish and more. Learn about the tides, reefs, dolphins and life cycles of sea turtles that nest on our local beaches. The center also offers guided beach walks, marsh treks and a gift shop full of fluffy critters to take home!

© Georgia State Parks

Commune with Nature

52 Diamond Causeway | 800.864.7275 | gastateparks.org/SkidawayIsland

Miles of hiking and biking trails wind through salt marshes and maritime forests within the 588 acres of **Skidaway Island State Park**. Whether your making it a day trip or pack the tent for a few days of camping, be on the lookout for the park's many animal residents, including deer, fiddler crabs, egrets and flocks of migrating birds. The interpretive center at the ranger's station has a birding station, a reptile room and other natural and cultural exhibits.

© Bryan Stovall

Explore a Fort

U.S. 80 East | 912.786.5787 | nps.gov/fopu

As you walk through the cannonball-shattered walls of **Fort Pulaski National Monument**, it's a cinch to imagine what it was like to guard the Savannah River way back when. Built in 1847, the fort was used by Confederacy and thought to be impenetrable until the Union Army tested its new rifled canon in 1862, rendering brick forts everywhere obsolete. After you've strolled through both levels, check out the visitors' center's films and live demonstrations as well as the moat, drawbridge and network of wooded trails. Keep your eyes peeled for a deer or a bald eagle—or, considering its haunted reputation, maybe even the ghost of a Confederate soldier.

© Savannah Sand Gnats

Catch a Fly Ball

1401 Victory Road | 912.351.9150 | sandgnats.com

Baseball legends Hank Aaron and Babe Ruth have scuffed their cleats at historic Grayson Stadium, home to the beloved **Savannah Sand Gnats**. A friendly crowd cheers for the home team while enjoying comfortable seating, gourmet treats and fireworks (the selection of microbrews make this an excellent grown-up outing, too!) Don't forget to high-five the team mascot, Gnate the Gnat.

© Old Town Trolley Tours of Savannah, Inc.

Earn a Badge

10 E. Oglethorpe Avenue | 912.233.4502 | girlscouts.org/birthplace

Welcome to the **Juliette Gordon Low Birthplace**, otherwise known as "Girl Scout Mecca." But you don't have to sport a sash to appreciate the legacy of a woman called "Daisy" who launched an organization to empower young girls and improve the world (the cookies came later.) Enthusiastic guides know every nook and cranny of the elegant 1821 home, furnished with 19th-century furniture and pieces from the family's collection.

See Science in Action

30 Ocean Science Circle | 912.598.2496 | marex.uga.edu.

The scientists at the **UGA Marine Education Center and Aquarium** on Skidaway Island are delighted to share their findings with visitors. A premier marine science research facility, the educational complex features 14 saltwater aquaria, interactive exhibits and a wheelchair accessible boardwalk around the marsh.

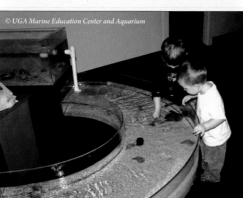
© UGA Marine Education Center and Aquarium

Make a Splash

Pirates Cove Water Park is slated for opening May 2011 near I-95 and Highway 204.

Though it's only just begun construction as this publication goes to print, **Pirates Cove Water Park** already has kids itching to get wet! With ten acres of pools, slides, an 18,000 square-foot surfing section and beach volleyball facilities, this is bound to be one Savannah's hottest spots.

© Mighty Eighth Air Force Museum

Fly a B-17 Bomber

175 Bourne Avenue in Pooler | 912.748.8888 | mightyeighth.org

Or least feel like you are: The interactive flight simulator at the **Mighty Eighth Air Force Museum** might make your dizzy with its engine roar and flashing cockpit. It's part of a dramatic 90,000 square-foot installation that was built to honor air force veterans of WWII and "edutain" generations about the heroics of these men and women. The second floor displays authentic war regalia, including a dog-tag machine, while the Combat Gallery boasts a fleet of restored aircraft used in battle, where you can at least stand next to a real B-17 Bomber.

© Bryan Stovall

Let Your Ears Ring

1 Fort Jackson Road | 912.232.3945 | chsgeorgia.org

Hear the awesome thunder of cannon fire at **Old Fort Jackson**, one of only eight "second system" fortifications built prior to the War of 1812 still standing in the U.S. The **Coastal Heritage Society** maintains the visitor's center featuring an exhibit of historical weapons and a host of highly-entertaining guides dressed in period garb. ❈

SAVANNAH Sand Gnats™

2011 SCHEDULE

	HOME		AWAY	
NORTHERN DIVISION			**SOUTHERN DIVISION**	
DEL	Delmarva Shorebirds		ASH	Asheville Tourists
GSO	Greensboro Grasshoppers		AUG	Augusta GreenJackets
HAG	Hagerstown Suns		CHA	Charleston Riverdogs
HIC	Hickory Crawdads		GRV	Greenville Drive
KAN	Kannapolis Intimidators		LEX	Lexington Legends
LAK	Lakewood BlueClaws		ROM	Rome Braves
WV	West Virginia Power		SAV	Savannah Sand Gnats

SANDGNATS.com

APRIL

Sunday	Monday	Tuesday	Wednesday	Thursday	Friday	Saturday
					1	2
3	4	5	6	7 WV	8 WV	9 WV
10 WV	11 HIC	12 HIC	13 HIC	14 HIC	15 GRV	16 GRV
17 GRV	18 GRV	19 LEX	20 LEX	21 LEX	22 LEX	23 LEX
24 DEL	25 DEL	26 DEL	27 DEL	28 DEL	29 DEL	30 LAK

MAY

Sunday	Monday	Tuesday	Wednesday	Thursday	Friday	Saturday
1 LAK	2 LAK	3 LAK	4	5 ROM	6 ROM	7 ROM
8 ROM	9 HIC	10 HIC	11 HIC	12 HIC	13 ROM	14 ROM
15 ROM	16 ROM	17 CHA	18 CHA	19 CHA	20 GRV	21 GRV
22 GRV	23 GRV	24	25 AUG	26 AUG	27 AUG	28 AUG
29 CHA	30 CHA	31 CHA				

JUNE

Sunday	Monday	Tuesday	Wednesday	Thursday	Friday	Saturday
			1 KAN	2 KAN	3 KAN	4 KAN
5 ASH	6 ASH	7 ASH	8	9 AUG	10 AUG	11 AUG
12 ROM	13 ROM	14 ROM	15 ROM	16 GRV	17 GRV	18 GRV
19 GRV	20	21	22	23 AUG	24 AUG	25
26 AUG	27 ROM	28 ROM	29 ROM	30 ROM		

JULY

Sunday	Monday	Tuesday	Wednesday	Thursday	Friday	Saturday
					1 AUG	2 AUG
3 AUG	4 ROM	5 ROM	6 ROM	7 GSO	8 GSO	9 GSO
10 GSO	11	12 LEX	13 LEX	14 LEX	15 LEX	16 AUG
17 AUG	18 AUG	19	20 WV	21 WV	22 WV	23 LEX
24 LEX	25 LEX	26 LEX	27	28 GSO	29 GSO	30 GSO
31 GSO						

AUGUST

Sunday	Monday	Tuesday	Wednesday	Thursday	Friday	Saturday
	1 AUG	2 AUG	3 AUG	4 AUG	5 CHA	6 CHA
7 CHA	8 CHA	9	10 GRV	11 GRV	12 GRV	13 GRV
14 ASH	15 ASH	16 ASH	17 ASH	18 GRV	19 GRV	20 GRV
21 GRV	22 ROM	23 ROM	24 ROM	25 ROM	26 CHA	27 CHA
28 CHA	29 CHA	30 CHA	31			

SEPTEMBER

Sunday	Monday	Tuesday	Wednesday	Thursday	Friday	Saturday
				1 LEX	2 LEX	3 LEX
4 LEX	5 LEX	6	7	8	9	10

© Bryan Stovall

Higher Education

COLLEGE-BOUND? HERE'S THE LOWCOUNTRY'S ACADEMIC LOWDOWN

By Jessica Leigh Lebos

Many folks come to Savannah to scout one of the area's esteemed institutions of higher learning. From fine arts to engineering to hospitality, there's a degree for every bright young mind.

Savannah College of Art and Design.   Known as SCAD throughout Savannah and beyond, this "center for creative careers" has earned an international reputation for providing gifted young people an education that nurtures artistic vision while providing the tools to make a living. President Paula Wallace was part of the original group that launched SCAD in 1979 and oversaw the purchase and renovation of many of Savannah's neglected historic buildings to use as classrooms and workshops, an effort that helped transform downtown Savannah into its current urban glory.

Today, the campus extends all over the city, from the **Gutstein Gallery** on Broughton Street to the **Gulfstream Center for Industrial Design** on south Barnard Street. In addition to its curricula in photography, film, fashion, fine arts, graphic design and other artistic disciplines, the university also boasts award-winning equestrian facilities and an accomplished athletic department, competing with men's and women's teams in 16 Sun NAIA conference sports. With a student body of 9,000 and sister campuses in Atlanta, Hong Kong and Lacoste, France, SCAD continues to take an energetic lead in education with its talented faculty, up-to-the-minute technologies and student support systems. *scad.edu.*

Armstrong Atlantic University.   A strong commitment to ideals of a broad, liberal education spurred the Aldermen of the City of Savannah to found Armstrong Junior College in 1935 on the far south end of town. The charming, tree-lined campus became a full-fledged university in 1996, where over 7,000 students a year from 70 different countries participate in **AASU**'s liberal arts tradition through study in the arts and sciences, teacher education, criminal justice, engineering, health professions—including a doctorate in physical therapy—and computer technology.

College life is more than just attending class, and students can find like-minded folks in over 80 different student organizations, including Greek life, faith-based groups and the Hispanic Outreach and Leadership Program. If sports is your bag, there's an active intramural team program, and the NCAA Division II men's and women's athletics teams are regular players in regional championships—be sure to keep your eye on men's baseball and women's tennis! *armstrong.edu.*

Savannah State University.   As the oldest historically black university in Georgia and the oldest institution of higher learning in Savannah, **SSU** takes great pride in its legacy of scholarship, research and community involvement. Its 173-acre campus has been housed since 1891 on a pristine salt-marsh estuary less than ten minutes from Savannah's downtown historic district and 20 minutes from the beach. Today, its diverse student body of 3,600 pursues 22 undergraduate and four graduate degrees in three colleges: Business Administration, Liberal Arts and Social Sciences and Sciences and Technology. Its Masters' of Marine Science is the only one of its kind in the Southeastern United States.

Students lead a classic campus life near the water with myriad organizations, options to join in the thriving Greek system and cheering for competitive NCAA Division I Athletics teams. The Marching Tigers Band is a grand spectacle not be missed at Tiger football games! *savannahstate.edu*.

Savannah Technical College. With a newly-renovated centralized Savannah campus and grand facilities in Liberty, Bryan and Effingham counties, **Savannah Tech** sets a high bar for trade and technical education. Offering over 50 certificates, diplomas and associate degrees, from automotive technology to marketing to historical preservation to solar energy systems installation, the college works closely with its business partners in the community to provide educational tools to build a strong workforce and enhance economic development.

Savannah Tech was recognized as one of the fastest-growing two-year colleges in the country, and recent attention has been garnered for Savannah Tech's culinary arts program: The Culinary Institute of Savannah's Hot Food Team earned a silver medal at the American Culinary Federation's national competition last year. *savannahtech.edu*.

South University. Established in 1899 in Savannah, **South University** currently oversees eight campuses around the country. The compact campus on Savannah's south side offers Associate's, Bachelor's, and Master's degree programs in business, criminal justice, graphic design, physician's assistant and other health professions, information technology, paralegal studies and nursing. There's also a top-notch doctorate program at the School of Pharmacy, and the school's library boasts cutting-edge law and medical research services. *southuniversity.edu*

Georgia Tech. One of Atlanta's finest universities opened up its Savannah Technology and Engineering campus in 2008, offering the intellectual standards of its big city counterpart with a more personalized atmosphere. Strong minds earn undergraduate and graduate degrees in the main engineering disciplines, including civil, mechanical, electrical and environmental engineering. The esteemed Georgia Tech presence has brought Savannah up to speed with other intellectual centers and continues to promote economic development by turning out engineers prepared to meet a technologically driven future. *gtsav.gatech.edu*

Georgia Southern. Located about an hour inland in lovely Statesboro, this full-service university and research facility is the largest educational institution in the southern half of the state.

Founded in 1908 as an agricultural school for rural children, Georgia Southern now boasts over 19,000 students in eight different colleges. Well-known for its outstanding athletics—including six NCAA football championships—has also amassed national acclaim for its 11-acre botanical gardens and its unique wildlife education center featuring diverse habitats and birds of prey. *georgiasouthern.edu*

University of South Carolina Beaufort. Just thirty minutes over the Talmadge Bridge across the South Carolina border, **USCB**'s South Campus offers high-quality baccalaureate degrees in the liberal arts as well as programs tailored specifically to the economic growth of the Lowcountry, including nursing and hospitality management. Students gain access to the area's rich heritage, including Gullah history, protected wetlands and island amenities. *uscb.edu* ❀

©University of South Carolina Beaufort

Opposite: The **Savannah College of Art and Design** has restored many of Savannah's historic buildings. *Above:* Students mingle at the **University of South Carolina Beaufort**.

What to do After Dark?

KICK UP YOUR HEELS OR COOL 'EM OFF WITH
EVERY KIND OF MUSIC UNDER THE MOON

By Patrick Rodgers

© Erin Adams Photography

Savannah may mind her manners during the day, but at night the old gal still knows how to ruffle a few petticoats. Whether you're looking to hoot and holler with the night owls or enjoy some jazz and a nightcap after a long day of shopping and museum tours, our city is more than happy to oblige you.

If you want to celebrate with a crowd, take a stroll along River Street and sample a little something for everyone. On the west end, **Livewire Music Hall** is a regular destination for jam bands, electronica artists and college radio rockers.

A short walk down the street, **The Warehouse** offers a steady stream of local rock acts, along with "the coldest beer in town." If you're in the mood for traditional Irish music, the friendly folks at **Kevin Barry's Irish Pub** are always ready to celebrate Savannah's strong Celtic traditions. Irish troubadours play seven nights a week in an acoustically-stunning music room—the mandolin never sounded so lovely.

Further north, away from the hustle and bustle is **Abe's on Lincoln**, an Old World-style pub with plenty of Guiness on tap. Speaking of taps, the **Moon River Brewing Company** on Bay Street has its own recipes flowing, along with a friendly brewpub atmosphere.

Another popular destination is City Market, which stretches from the newly restored Ellis Square west to Franklin Square. Check out **Wild Wing Café**, where there's live music inside and out on

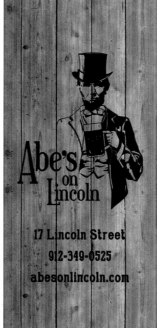

the weekends. Just a few feet further brings you to the subterranean **Bar Bar**, which features two bars, pool and foosball tables and an always-packed dance floor. To drink among friends in the open air, climb the stairs to the **Roof Top Tavern**.

Around the corner is Congress Street, home to some Savannah's liveliest nightlife. In short order, you'll find **Bacchus Wine Bar**, which features DJs spinning all genres of dance music, and **Molly MacPherson's**, a Scottish Pub with one of the best selections of single malt Scotch in the city.

A few blocks east will bring you to **The Jinx**, a live music club featuring outlaw country, metal and rockabilly, as well as some of the city's best tattoos. Right next door, you'll find **Mercury Lounge**, one of the best spots to hear live electric blues in the city as well as a basement with darts and shuffleboard.

There are a couple of karaoke bars downtown should you need to indulge your inner diva. On the river, swing by **Bernie's**, a raw bar by day that starts cooking at night with some of the liveliest karaoke in town. If you're further, make a stop at **McDonough's** at the corner of Drayton and McDonough streets, which offers DIY singing opportunities seven nights a week.

If something smooth is what you're after, head over to the **Planter's Tavern** in the basement of the **Olde Pink House**, where two large fireplaces and great piano jazz light up the intimate space. Another spot that lives up to its moniker is **Jazz'd**, a tapas restaurant well-known for its martinis, industrial-chic décor and steady stream of great live jazz and blues. For more great jazz, check out **Sugar Daddy's**, a wine bar featuring Savannah's only pure jazz jam every Tuesday night and all kinds of music the rest of the week.

If dancing accompanied by wine or some champagne is more your style, drop by **Saya**, where DJs spin a steady stream of mash-ups, house and Top 40 faves in an underground spot with a chic, Far East vibe. Or try **Seed**, an eco-lounge with the same musical M.O., but with a focus on organic vodkas and sleek décor.

When your sweet tooth starts to beckon, take a trip to **Lulu's Chocolate Bar** on Martin Luther King Jr. Boulevard, where the owners offer up a selection of homemade treats, after-dinner drinks and specially-crafted martinis.

For great indie rock, folk and electronica without all the hassle of a bar, check the listings at **The Sentient Bean**, a progressive-minded coffeeshop on the south end of **Forsyth Park**, which regularly hosts emerging local and touring acts—not to mention a line-up of quirky movie screenings, spoken word and art openings. If you're in the mood for something more theatrical, check out **Muse Arts Warehouse**, a black box theater on Louisville Road that hosts plays, live music and comedy.

You might have thought it was hot during the day, but that's nothing once you've seen how cool it is in Savannah once the sun goes down. ❧

© Visit Savannah

Celebrations for All Seasons

Savannah hosts over 200 festivals each year celebrating the arts, culture, holidays and more. Here are the highlights:

Savannah Black Heritage Festival

February 1–13, 2011 | savannahblackheritagefestival.com

African-American art, gospel music and Gullah-Geechee storytelling entertain while health-related and economic programming inform. Events take place all over the city; don't miss a talk with prize-winning children's book author and puppet maker Ashley Bryan and a spectacular performance with all-female *a cappella* ensemble Sweet Honey in the Rock.

Georgia History Festival

February 1-12, 2011 | georgiahistory.com

Held annually around the anniversary of the founding of the colony of Georgia in February 1733, this lively two-week commemoration brings history to life for all ages. The 2011 schedule includes crafts workshops, the Colonial Faire and Muster at **Wormsloe State Historic Site**, the colorful Georgia Day parade, Super Museum Sunday and the Trustees Gala where the governor will induct this year's Georgia Trustees, legendary UGA football coach Vince Dooley and global policy maker Senator Sam Nunn.

Savannah Book Festival

February 18-21, 2011 | savannahbookfestival.org

Literati from near and far convene at Telfair Square for lectures, book signings and workshops led leaders in all the top genres: Fiction, history, biography, poetry and beyond. Check the website to see if your favorite author is making an appearance; you'll see that the SBF hosts events all year long, including an evening with best-selling mystery author Stuart Woods and a musical tribute to Pulitzer Prize-winning Southerner Eudora Welty.

Savannah Music Festival

March 24-April 9, 2011 | savannahmusicfestival.org

From *avant garde* jazz and bluegrass to symphonic classics to rock n' roll, the SMF leaves no aural stone unturned. Renowned internationally for its breadth of scope and quality of artists, the multiple stages have featured the likes of Stuart Copeland, Bela Fleck, Wilco, Angelique Kidjo and Savannah's own Ben Tucker. SMF commissions original work each year, premiering pieces by global artists heard publically for the first time in Savannah.

© Frank Stewart

© C.R. Murray Photography, Travis Sayre & Nancy Heffernan

Savannah Craft Brew Fest

September 2-3, 2011 | savannahcraftbrewfest.com

These folks elevate beer drinking to an art form when over 120 microbrew companies bring their wares to the Savannah International Trade & Convention Center Labor Day Weekend. Brews are matched with the finest Lowcountry cuisine to bring out their best flavors at the Craft Brew Pairings Dinner on Friday night, followed by an all-day bonanza Saturday with entertainment, excellent eats and of course, plenty of taxis so no one needs to drive home.

Savannah Jazz Festival

September 18-25, 2011 | savannahjazzfestival.org

Savannah always cools off for fall with a week of free music events sponsored by the city, most taking place on the amphitheater stage in Forsyth Park. From Dixieland and swing to downhome "gutbucket" blues and the swirly stylings of modern contemporary masters, Jazzfest brings together every genre to appeal to all ages and tastes. No need for tickets—just grab a cooler and a folding chair and you're good to go!

Tybee Island Pirate Festival

October 2011 (check website for exact dates) | tybeeisland.com/piratefest

Arrrgh ya ready for some marauding and mischief?! Tybee Island celebrates the high-flying antics of history's friendly buccaneers with a weekend of treasure hunting at the Thieves' Market, a costumed gala, activities for the little mates, a parade where pirates share their booty with the crowd and a music festival that the likes of that ye landlubbers have ne'er experienced.

Savannah Film Festival

October 2011 (check website for exact dates) | filmfest.scad.edu

The Savannah College of Art and Design brings Hollywood to Savannah with screenings of the best independent films from around the world. Big-time directors share screen time with student filmmakers to showcase shorts, features and documentaries, many of which go on to become box office smashes. Celebrities tend to find their way to town during this time, transforming Savannah into Los Angeles for short while, paparazzi and all.

River Street Festivals

Throughout 2011 | riverstreetsavannah.com

No matter what time of year, River Street has a festival to celebrate: **First Friday** fireworks bring new meaning to TGIF, followed by the family fun and bustling art scene of **First Saturdays**. Practically every culture gets its due on the historic cobblestoned street through the seasons, from the German food and songs of **Oktoberfest** to June's spicy **Fiesta Latina** to the one of the biggest, greenest **St. Patrick's Day** celebrations in the nation. **Fine Arts on the River** showcases visual and performing arts, and **Christmas on the River** is as a fine a Savannah tradition as they come. Events are always family-friendly!

—JLL

Savannah *Festivals & Events* for 2011

January

MLK, Jr. Observance Day Celebration
912.234.5502 · savannahga.gov

Savannah Hockey Classic
912.644.6414 · SavannahVisit.com

February

Super Museum Sunday
912.651.2125 · georgiahistory.com

Savannah Irish Festival
912.232.3448 · savannahirish.org

March

Tara Feis Festival
912.651.6417 · savannahga.gov

Tybee's St. Patrick's Heritage Celebration
912.786.5444 · tybeevisit.com

St. Patrick's Day Parade and Celebration
912.233.4804 · savannahsaintpatricksday.com

Savannah Tour of Homes and Gardens
912.234.8054 · savannahtourofhomes.org

April

Savannah Garden Exposition
912.236.4795 · savannahgardenexpo.com

N.O.G.S. Tour of Hidden Gardens
912.961.4805 · gcofsavnogstour.org

Liberty Mutual Legends of Golf Tournament
912.236.1333 · lmlog.com

May

Fine Arts on the River Festival
912.234.0295 · riverstreetsavannah.com

SCAD Sidewalk Arts Festival
912.525.5231 · scad.edu

SCAD Sand Arts Festival
912.525.5231 · scad.edu

Savannah Scottish Games
912.233.6017 · savannahscottishgames.com

Tybee Island Beach Bum Parade
912.786.5444 · tybeevisit.com

June

Armed Forces Festival on River Street
912.234.0295 · riverstreetsavannah.com

Savannah Asian Festival
912.651.6417 · savannahga.gov

Festival Latina
912.651.6417 · savannahga.gov

July

Fourth of July on the River
912.234.0295 · riverstreetsavannah.com

Fourth of July Fireworks on the Beach
912.786.5444 · tybeevisit.com

ArtSquared Savannah
912.644.6452 · SavannahVisit.com

August

Blue vs. Gray End of Summer Celebration
912.786.5787 · nps.gov/fopu

Labor Day Beach Bash
912.786.5393 · tybeefest.com

September

Savannah Craft Brew Fest
savannahcraftbrewfest.com

Taste of Savannah
912.232.1223 · www.tourismleadershipcouncil.com

October

Oktoberfest on the River
912.234.0295 · riverstreetsavannah.com

Savannah Folk Music Festival
912.786.6953 · savannahfolk.org

Savannah Greek Festival
912.236.8256 · stpaul.ga.goarch.org

Tybee Festival of the Arts
912.786.5920 · tybeearts.org/festival

St. Vincent's Academy Tour of Homes & Tea
912.819.7780 · svatourofhomes.com

Shalom Y'all Jewish Food Festival
912.233.1547 · mickveisrael.org

November

Savannah Seafood Festival
912.234.0295 · riverstreetsavannah.com

Telfair Art Fair
912.790.8800 · telfair.org

Savannah Holly Days
912.644.6452 · savannahhollydays.com

Savannah Harbor Boat Parade of Lights
912.201.2000 · westinsavannah.com

December

ENMARK Savannah River Bridge Run
912.355.3527 · savannahriverbridgerun.com

Christmas On the River and Lighted Holiday Parade
912.234.0295 · riverstreetsavannah.com

City Market Christmas for Kids Celebration
912.232.4903 · savannahcitymarket.com

Holiday Tour of Homes
912.236.8362 · dnaholidaytour.com

City Market Holiday Open House
912.232.4903 · savannahcitymarket.com

Tybee New Year's Eve Fireworks
912.786.5444 · tybeevisit.com

City Market New Year's Eve Celebration
912.232.4903 · savannahcitymarket.com

For a more comprehensive listing of all Savannah events, please go to www.VisitSavannah.com.

Savannah's Historic Riverfront!

Historic River Street · Factors Walk · Bay Street · Hutchinson Island

Dine · Shop · Play · Stay

January 1	New Year's Eve Fireworks on the River		August 5	First Friday Fireworks on the River
February 4	First Friday Fireworks on the River		August 6	First Saturday on the River
March 4	First Friday Fireworks on the River		September 2	First Friday Fireworks on the River
March 5	First Saturday on the River		September 3, 4	River Street Labor Day Celebration
March 17-19	St. Patrick's Day on the River		Sept. 30 - Oct. 2	Oktoberfest on the River
April 1	First Friday Fireworks on the River		November 4	First Friday Fireworks on the River
April 2	First Saturday on the River		November 5	First Saturday on the River
April 22-24	Fine Arts on the River		November 11-13	Savannah Land, Sea & Air Show
May 7	First Saturday on the River		November 26	Savannah Harbor Boat Parade of Lights
May 20-22	Armed Forces Festival		December 2	First Friday Fireworks on the River
June 3	First Friday Fireworks on the River		December 3, 4	Christmas on the River
June 4	First Saturday on the River		December 3	Lighted Christmas Parade
July 2, 3, 4	Great American Weekend & July 4 Fireworks		January 1	New Year's Eve Fireworks on the River

912.234.0295 | **RiverStreetSavannah.com**

Just Relax

A spa connossieur shares her favorite indulgences

By Gloria Greenbaum

©Westin Savannah Harbor Golf Resort and Spa

©Magnolia Spa

Above left: Serenity awaits at **Heavenly Spa at the Westin Savannah Harbor Golf Resort & Spa**. *Above right:* Steam away the stress at **Magnolia Spa at Savannah Marriott Riverfront.**

Listen, dahlin', you've been on your feet all day with all the sightseeing and shopping. You deserve some relaxation.

Time to put on a fluffy robe and let the experts pamper you from top to bottom. As a local who doesn't let a week go by without a visit to one of our fabulous spas, I must encourage you to follow in my well-pedicured footsteps:

Savannah is world-class is so many ways, and as someone who follows her husband on business trips around the globe, I can attest that the massages at **Heavenly Spa at the Westin Savannah Harbor Golf Resort & Spa** are even better than those I've had from the little ladies who walk on your back in Thailand. Whenever I'm feeling fatigued, I check in for a River Rock Therapy massage—the hot stones gently release my stress and balance my energy centers. If you're feeling parched, the Heavenly Body restorative treatment with its kamani oil and orange juniper serum will leave your skin smooth and as young-looking as a teenager's!

The massage services at **Magnolia Spa at the Savannah Marriott Riverfront** are also divine, though my favorite way to play here is with a L'Athene Signature Anti-Aging facial—because let's face it, forty is pretty far back in my rearview mirror and I can use all the help I can get. For four hours of total submission to your own loveliness, sign on for the Magnolia treatment—a full-session massage, facial, manicure and pedicure to transform every cuticle, cell and pore.

The body therapies offered at the **Posiedon Spa** inside the **Mansion at Forsyth Park** are so relaxing they border on the transcendental (and I should know, since I've spent plenty of time spa-hopping in India last year.) The exfoliating Hydro Body Polish begins with the healing waters of their Vichy shower and ends with moisturizing lotions, and the Oceanic Detoxifying Wrap with its vitamin-packed healing soak is the perfect thing after one too many bottles of Cristal.

When I'm feeling homesick for Venice but don't need the hassle of all those darn canals, I simply have my personal assistant book me some time at **Terme Acqua Dolce**, also known as **Sweet Water Spa**. My hands and feet always receive royal treatment here with an Ultimate Mani/Pedi, which includes a milk and honey soak and microdermabrasion exfoliation. And I just adore sitting in those throne-like chairs—it reminds me that I am the queen of my own life!

Of course, all of the above offer services especially for the kings in our lives. To thank my husband for all his hard work and keeping me in the luxurious style to which I've become accustomed (and don't ever plan to change), I tell his secretary to make us a lunch date at the **Savannah Day Spa**, where he succumbs to a private steam, massage, mani/pedi and shave and haircut. He especially likes that he comes out smelling like a man—the sage and sandalwood scent is his favorite.

Now, I am still working my way through the menus at all of these spas, but those are my current recommendations for an hour or two of bliss—though there's nothing wrong with combining a few services to take up the entire afternoon …

An Eternal *Romance*

This is a city that invites intimacy. Lacy curtains of moss drape ancient oaks. Flowers bloom throughout the seasons, sending out delicate fragrance. The evening air is sultry, occasionally ruffling one's hair with a breeze off the river. An empty bench for two seems to beckon, eager to serve as the setting for a first kiss—or an embrace celebrating a lifetime of love.

©Angela Hopper Photography

For information on planning your wedding, anniversary or honeymoon, go to *SavannahIDo.com*.

Savannah has long enjoyed her reputation as one of America's most romantic cities. Her glorious architecture, cobblestone pathways and burbling fountains have impressed even the most cynical minds: At the end of the Civil War, General Sherman was in the midst of leading his Union Army on a burning rampage that destroyed many other Southern cities on its March to the Sea. When the grizzled general arrived in Savannah, he was so taken with her charm that he gave orders to his soldiers to put down their torches—and promptly sent a telegram to President Lincoln presenting the intact beauty of Savannah as a Christmas gift.

So perhaps it's the preservation of antebellum history that lends Savannah its soft glow. Or maybe it's just the way the sun dapples through the magnolia trees. Whatever the magic is, many a couple has been enchanted with this jewel of the South.

Savannah has indeed become one of the most popular wedding destinations in the world in the past few years, on par with big cities and tropical locales. Dream weddings find their way into reality here with a thriving industry of professionals specifically catering to a bride and groom's vision of their perfect day—be it exchanging vows in a gazebo on the square before being whisked away in a horse-drawn carriage or declaring their eternal love while barefoot on the beach.

Honeymoons, anniversaries or just-for-fun jaunts are also excellent reasons to share Savannah with your favorite person. Enjoy each other's company as you spend the days exploring shops and museums then wile away the nights at world-class restaurants and cozy pubs.

Walk in the footsteps of so many contented couples that have come before. After all, what more fortuitous a place to cultivate a long and happy romance than a place that's stood the test of time? —JLL

©Richard Leo Johnson

©Bryan Stovall

Art Around Every Corner

From classic to contemporary, museums and galleries offer a feast for the eyes and soul

By Allison Hersh

Georgia's First City warmly embraces the arts, nurturing emerging talent and celebrating the visual arts. With a range that encompasses everything from 18th-century portraiture to black-and-white photography to wild multi-media installations, the entire city is a palette, inside and out.

Savannah has emerged as a national haven for creativity. In fact, the arts scene has grown steadily over the last decade, anchored by the Savannah College of Art and Design's success and fueled by a growing appetite for original work by talented local artists. Art lovers can discover a wide array of styles, media and approaches that rival treasures found in established art meccas like New York or Santa Fe.

MAIN ATTRACTIONS

Savannah's art museums are home to a number of world-class collections. From folk art to photography, visitors can enjoy something for every taste. Here are a few must-see stops for anyone with a passion for the visual arts.

Jepson Center for the Arts

207 W. York Street | 912.790.8800 | telfair.org

This sleek glass and marble museum overlooking Telfair Square serves as the epicenter for contemporary art in Savannah. With galleries dedicated to Southern art, African-American art, photography and traveling exhibits, the Jepson Center delights art aficionados of all ages.

In addition, the Jepson Center also is home to a popular hands-on ArtZeum for kids, which includes commissioned works by glass artist Therman Statom and computer-video artist Daniel Shiffman. Children can learn about art through interactive, hands-on exploration, playing with a magnetic sculpture wall, building architectural structures with wooden pieces or experimenting with video art installations.

Telfair Academy

121 Barnard Street | 912.790.8800 | telfair.org

Want to see the legendary "Bird Girl" statue that graces the cover of John Berendt's best-seller, *Midnight in the Garden of Good and Evil*? You'll find Sylvia Shaw Judson's iconic statue on permanent display at the Telfair Academy, where it had to be relocated after visitors overcrowded Bonaventure Cemetery, the Bird Girl's original location, in the wake of *Midnight's* success.

The oldest art museum in the South, the Telfair also features an impressive Sculpture Gallery, a dramatic Rotunda accented with works from the museum's permanent collection, and period rooms showcasing a world-class decorative arts collection with a rare American and European antiques. Highlights from the permanent collection include stunning examples of American Impressionism, Ashcan School painting and the largest public collection of visual art in North America by poet Kahlil Gibran, best known as author of *The Prophet*.

"For its size, Savannah is an extremely creative community," raves Steven High, director of the Telfair Museum of Art. "There's a great artistic energy here."

Beach Institute

502 E. Harris Street | 912.234.8000 | kingtisdell.org

This historic 1867 building, originally built to encourage African-American education in Savannah, houses an extensive collection of imaginative folk art by Ulysses Davis (1913-1990), a legendary Savannah woodcarver. The Ulysses Davis Collection, which is on permanent display at the Beach Institute, features a selection of sculptures by this self-taught African-American artist, including a complete collection of wooden sculptures devoted to each of America's Presidents.

Davis's sculptures have been featured at the Corcoran Gallery of Art in Washington, D.C., the High Museum of Art in Atlanta and the Library of Congress in Washington, D.C. Much of his work deals with spiritual themes and reveals a rich influence from African tribal art.

SCAD Museum of Art

Kiah Hall | 227 MLK Jr. Boulevard | 912.525.7191 | scad.edu

Dedicated in 2002, the SCAD Museum of Art exhibits a wide selection of paintings, photography and mixed media work throughout the year. Showcasing nearly 4,500 objects, the museum is located in the former headquarters of the Central of Georgia Railroad, a restored 1856 Greek Revival treasure.

The SCAD Museum of Art features three major collections on permanent display: The Walter O. Evans Collection, which includes original work by African-American artists including Romare Bearden, Aaron Douglas and Jacob Lawrence; the Earle W. Newton Center for British and American Studies, which features 200+ paintings ranging from the early 17th century to the mid-19th century; and the Shirrel Rhoades Photographic Collection, which boasts 135 photographs by Ansel Adams, Annie Leibovitz, Karl Lagerfeld, Imogen Cunningham and Richard Avedon.

©Bryan Stovall

©SCAD

Opposite left: The modern lines of the **Jepson Center for the Arts** were designed by architect Moshe Safdie. *Opposite right:* Peruse classic art at the **Telfair Academy**. *(see ad - page 98) Top:* The **Beach Institute** displays the work of folk artist Ulysses Davis. *Bottom:* Over 4,500 works are showcased at the **SCAD Museum of Art**.

Top: Buy locally-made art created by talented students at **shopSCAD**.
Bottom: Unique glasswork and contemporary paintings don the walls of **Chroma Gallery** near **Ellis Square**.

GALLERIES & CAFES

Savannah's galleries and cafés feature talent by local, regional and national artists. Here are a few places where you can find original treasures to add to your own collection.

The Art Center at City Market

Jefferson St. at W. St. Julian Street | 912.232.4903 | savannahcitymarket.com

Traditional and contemporary influences meet sparkle and whimsy among the dozens of galleries and studios that make up this community of artists and craftsmen. Observe painters, sculptors and textile artists at work in dozens of studios. There are even more galleries along City Market's open-air walkways—an entire day can be spent exploring this historic site known as "The Art and Soul of Savannah." Free and open to the public.

Chroma Gallery

31 Barnard Street | 912.232.2787 | chromaartgallery.com

Named after the Greek word for color, Chroma Gallery near City Market serves as living proof that collecting art can be fun. Founded 2001 by artists Jan Clayton Pagratis and Lori Keith Robinson, the gallery features vibrant paintings, hand-blown glass and creative jewelry by contemporary artists and artisans with roots in the Southeast.

Red Gallery

201 E. Broughton Street | 912.525.473 | scad.edu

This showcase Savannah College of Art and Design gallery always has something interesting to see. Works by artists ranging from Rembrandt to Andy Warhol have been featured here, often alongside compositions by SCAD students, faculty and alumni. Exhibits rotate frequently throughout the year.

shopSCAD

340 Bull Street | 912.525.5180 | shopscadonline.com

This Savannah College of Art and Design gallery and boutique specializes in hand-crafted items, from mixed media to paintings to quilts, by SCAD students and alumni. With a wide range of prices, Shop SCAD serves as a great place to find creative, unique gifts.

Gallery Espresso

234 Bull Street | 912.233.5348 | galleryespresso.com

One of the city's best venues for emerging artists, this bustling café serves as an excellent launching point for many local painters and photographers. A great place to catch a rising star.

Sentient Bean

13 E. Park Avenue | 912.232.4447 | sentientbean.com

This laid-back, free trade coffee house features art exhibits all year-round, many of which focus on themes relating to the environment, social justice and peace. An affordable community gallery with a conscience.

THE ART CENTER AT CITY MARKET

Art Galleries

A.T. Hun Gallery	302 W. St. Julian Street	912.233.2060
Jim Pennington Fine Art	307 W. St. Julian Street	985.789.5547
Raffine Galerie	306 W. Congress Street	912.232.6400
Signature Gallery	303 W. St. Julian Street	912.233.3082
Stephen Kasun Gallery	305-A W. Bryan Street	407.474.0411
The Gallery	20 Jefferson Street	912.231.2025
Thomas Kinkade Gallery	211 W. St. Julian Street	912.447.4660

City Market Art Center Studios *(912.232.4903)*

Addiktspace Studios *Nelson/Stavella/Larsen Art Studio*	308 W. St. Julian St. - *Upper Level Studio FNU-106*	
Albert Seidl	308 W. St. Julian St. - *Upper Level Studio FNU-110*	912.665.1485
Brian MacGregor	308 W. St. Julian St. - *Upper Level Studio FNU-104*	912.596.2201
Dennis Roth	309 W. St. Julian St. - *Upper Level, Studio FSU-4*	912.220.2234
Diane's Knitting Studio	308 W. St. Julian St. - *Upper Level Studio FNU-108*	912.441.9020
Dottie Farrell & Bess Ramsey	309 W. St. Julian St. - *Upper Level, Studio FSU-1*	912.341.0122
Ga11ery 11	309 W. St. Julian St. - *Upper Level, Studio FSU-11*	912.441.2093
Gallery 10 - Pamella Dykema	309 W. St. Julian St. - *Upper Level, Studio FSU-10*	912.429.5326
Gallery 9 - Sue Gouse	309 W. St. Julian St. - *Upper Level, Studio FSU-9*	912.667.4378
Jim Holmes Photography	309 W. St. Julian St. - *Upper Level, Studio FSU-7*	912.354.8234
John Mitchell	309 W. St. Julian St. - *Upper Level, Studio FSU-1A*	912.308.1296
Julio Contreras	308 W. St. Julian St. - *Upper Level Studio FNU-105*	
Kerry Harried	309 W. St. Julian St. - *Upper Level, Studio FSU-2*	912.224.6925
King David	308 W. St. Julian St. - *Upper Level Studio FNU-107*	912.441.9040
Gallery 5	309 W. St. Julian St. - *Upper Level, Studio FSU-5*	912.659.1702
Osibisa Fine Arts - William Kwamena-Poh	309 W. St. Julian St. - *Upper Level, Studio FSU-8*	912.201.9009
Roeder Kinkel Studio	308 W. St. Julian St. - *Upper Level Studio FNU-109*	912.332.9082
Ruth Hunter Studio - Inner Landscapes	315 W. St. Julian St. - *FNU-101*	912.202.3041
Satori Handcrafted Art	308 W. St. Julian St. - *Upper Level Studio FNU-102*	912.598.9208
Savannah Blue Art Studio	308 W. St. Julian St. - *Upper Level Studio FNU-103*	912.790.1232
Susie Chisholm/Sculptor	309 W. St. Julian St. - *Upper Level, Studio FSU-6*	912.441.6261

www.savannahcitymarket.com/art

THE ART CENTER at City Market is a community of working artists who make and sell their work in a series of studios and galleries.

See 35 artists at work in the studio lofts.

912.232.4903 • SavannahCityMarket.com
309/315 W. St. Julian Street (upstairs)

©Kevin Nightingale

Homage to History

EXPLORE SAVANNAH'S PAST THROUGH MUSEUMS AND MEMORIALS

By Jessica Leigh Lebos

From the day in 1733 when General James Oglethorpe stepped upon the bluff and declared the colony of Georgia, the city of Savannah has been making history. Almost three centuries of important events and key historical figures are covered throughout downtown, from the Revolution of 1776 to the War of 1812, the Civil War to the Civil Rights Movement, our heroic soldiers to our favorite hometown crooner.

MUSEUMS

The Savannah History Museum

303 MLK Jr. Boulevard | 912.651.6825 | chsgeorgia.org

Housed within the former Central of Georgia Railroad passenger shed, the museum is adjacent to several other managed by the Coastal Heritage Society. Boasting over 10,000 artifacts relating to early Georgia and coastal history, the exhibits include weapons dating back the Revolutionary War, a rare Native American dugout canoe, a fabulous display of women's hats and 20th-century treasures like an Oscar® won by music man Johnny Mercer and the iconic bench used in the film *Forrest Gump*, filmed in Savannah.

The Ralph Mark Gilbert Civil Rights Museum

460 MLK Jr. Blvd., 912.231.8900, savcivilrights.com

Within the former Wage Earners Savings & Loan bank built in 1914, three floors of interactive and photographic exhibits tell the story of the struggle and triumph of Georgia's oldest African-American community. Learn how the citizens of Savannah took Dr. King's philosophy of non-violence to heart and influenced city and business leaders to achieve equal rights during one of the most tumultuous times in our nation's history.

©Bryan Stovall

©Savannah History Museum

Opposite: The **Haitian Monument** commemorates the Chasseurs-Volontaires de Saint-Domingue who fought in the American Revolution. *Above:* Kids love the artifacts at the **Savannah History Museum**. *(see ad - page 65)* *Top right:* Nautical buffs should not miss the **Ships of the Sea Museum**.

Ships of the Sea Maritime Museum

41 MLK Jr. Boulevard | 912.232.1511 | shipsofthesea.org

The epic era of cross-Atlantic trade during the 18th and 19th centuries is given proper due at this exquisite museum housed in the elegant Scarborough House and its surrounding gardens. Handcrafted models of ships (including one of the first steamship to complete the Atlantic passage), exceptional paintings of maritime life and antiques hearkening back to a time when captains depended on the stars for nautical guidance make this a must-see for anyone who's ever had a dream of sailing adventure.

Georgia Historical Society

501 Whitaker Street | 912.651.2125 | georgiahistory.com

Presiding over the northwest corner of Forsyth Park, stately Hodgson Hall has been home to Georgia's oldest cultural institution since 1876. Researchers and bibliophiles use this jewel of a library to examine its millions of manuscripts, photographs, maps and architectural blueprints for academic as well as genealogical pursuits. In addition to providing stewardship over Georgia history in the city where it all began, GHS also provides educational programming and publishes a magazine, *Georgia History Today*, and an academic journal, *Georgia Historical Quarterly*. The Society also has offices in Atlanta and manages the thousands of historical markers throughout the state.

OUTDOOR MEMORIALS

African-American Monument *(W. River Street—behind the Hyatt Regency Savannah)*
This elevated sculpture of a family of four embracing as the chains of slavery lay broken at their feet recognizes the tragedies of slavery and the contributions to the city of Savannah made by African-American ancestors. Constructed in 2002 by SCAD professor Dorothy Spradley, the monument features an inscription composed by legendary poet Maya Angelou.

Waving Girl Statue *(E. River Street – near the Marriott Savannah Riverfront)*
One of Savannah's most familiar works of art, The Waving Girl statue honors Florence Martus (1869-1943), who waved a cloth by day and a lantern by night to ships sailing in and out of Savannah's port for nearly 40 years. According to local legend, she was always searching for her one-time love, a sailor who had promised to return to Savannah but never did. Nestled along Savannah's brick river walk, this bronze statue depicts Florence waving to passing ships, with her faithful dog by her side. *(right)*

Haitian Monument *(Franklin Square, Montgomery Street and W. Congress Street)*
Did you know that Haitian soldiers played a decisive role in the American Revolution, fighting in a pivotal battle in Savannah? The Haitian Monument in Franklin Square serves as a tribute to the Chasseurs-Volontaires de Saint-Domingue, a regiment of soldiers who battled the Brits in 1779. Consisting of more than 700 free men of color from the Island of Haiti, this regiment was the largest unit of men of African descent to fight in the American Revolution. The monument depicts six soldiers, including a drummer boy who represents young Henri Christophe who later became the king of Haiti.

©Kevin Nightingale

©Kevin Nightingale

WWII Monument *(W. River Street—near the Hyatt Regency Savannah)*
The soldiers of America's greatest generation receive due respect for their courage and sacrifice through this awe-inspiring homage dedicated in November 2010. Designed by Eric Meyerhoff, the copper globe split in two represents the theme "A World Apart" and stands 20 feet high. On the walk-through between the two parts are the names the Savannah-area men and women whose lives were lost in World War II.

Olympic Statue *(E. River Street—near the Marriott Savannah Riverfront)*
In 1996, Savannah proudly hosted the Olympic yachting events, which united some of the world's fastest sailboat racers. The Olympic torch passed through Savannah, invigorating the community and filling Savannah with price. Today, a massive bronze statue commemorates the eternal Olympic flame, which "burns" atop a base of Greek-inspired columns. The statue is located adjacent to the Waving Girl statue on the bluff overlooking the Savannah River. *(left)*

Johnny Mercer Sculpture *(Ellis Square, Barnard Street and W. Congress Street)*
Savannahians are proud of our newest outdoor sculpture, a life-sized bronze statue of Academy Award®-winning Savannah lyricist Johnny Mercer graces Ellis Square near City Market. Unveiled in November 2009 on what would have been Mercer's 100th birthday, the sculpture was meticulously crafted by local sculptor Susie Chisholm and reveals the songwriter behind such legendary songs as "Moon River" and "Days of Wine and Roses" in a relaxed moment, reading a newspaper and wearing a fedora. The statue is nestled along a public walkway, welcoming visitors to the square.

Flower Power

Savannah's temperate climate means something's always a'bloom.
Check out the year 'round calendar of vibrant color.

❧ **December-February:** *Camellias*

These dense, dark-leaved evergreen trees form pom-poms in late fall that burst into round, rose-shaped flowers throughout the winter. The flowers can be pink, red, yellow, white or variegated and come in single and double blooms. The most popular species found in Savannah gardens are *Camellia japonica* and *Camellia sasanqua.*

❧ **March-April:** *Azaleas*

Though it's impossible to predict exactly when it will happen, at sometime point in the early spring Savannah literally explodes with color, thanks to these ubiquitous shrubs. Filling the medians, sidewalks and squares with shades of purple, red, coral, white and pink, "Azalea-mania" lasts for two to three weeks and usually coincides with several garden tours and festivals. It is truly a spectacle to behold!

❧ **May-June:** *Gardenias*

These heat-loving plants begin to put out highly-fragrant flowers in early summer and often gear up for another bloom in late fall. The delicate, velvety white petals unfurl as a spiral and turn creamy yellow with age. Pluck one (with permission, of course) and float in a bowl of water to fill an entire room with a delightful scent.

❧ **May-July:** *Star Jasmine*

This clinging vine adorns Savannah's arbors, balconies and even mailboxes, throwing forth small, sweet-smelling clusters of white flowers during the early summer. Though often referred to as "Confederate jasmine," the evergreen is not native to the American South but to China.

❧ **June-July:** *Magnolias*

Each summer, these tall, stately trees with their waxy, brown-bottom leaves turn out white blossoms, infusing the air with a lemon-sugar scent. The bigger the tree, the larger the blossoms—some have the circumference of dinner plates!

❧ **June-September:** *Crape Myrtles*

The heat of summer brings out clouds of lavender, pink, maroon and white to fill the smooth gray branches of Savannah's many crape myrtle trees. After the tiny flowers peak, the leaves begin their own gorgeous showing of hues, turning shades of cinnamon-red, dusty pink and mustard yellow before they fall and the trees begin another beautiful cycle. —JLL

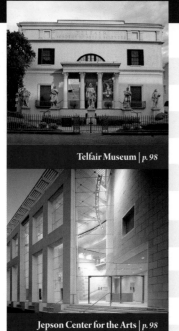

Telfair Museum | *p. 98*

Jepson Center for the Arts | *p. 98*

Savannah Sand Gnats | *p. 7, 77*

Savannah Riverfront | *p. 83*

Abe's on Lincoln	**912.349.0525**	**17 Lincoln Street**	**abesonlincoln.com**
The Art Center at City Market	**912.232.4903**	**Jefferson St. at W. St. Julian St.**	**savannahcitymarket.com/art/listing**
ArtZeum	**912.790.8800**	**207 W. York Street**	**telfair.org**
A.T. Hun Gallery	**912.233.2060**	**302 W. St. Julian Street**	**savannahcitymarket.com**
Beach Institute	912.234.8000	502 E. Harris Street	kingtisdell.org/beachinst
Chroma Gallery	912.232.2787	31 Barnard Street	chromaartgallery.com
City Market	**912.232.4903**	**219 W. Bryan Street, Suite 207**	**savannahcitymarket.com**
Civil Rights Museum	912.231.8900	460 MLK Jr. Boulevard	savcivilrights.com
Coastal Heritage Society	**912.651.6840**	**303 MLK Jr. Boulevard**	**chsgeorgia.org**
Fort Pulaski National Monument	912.786.5787	U.S. Hwy. 80 E. *(towards Tybee Island)*	nps.gov/fopu
The Gallery	**912.231.2025**	**20 Jefferson Street**	**thegallerysavannah.com**
Gallery Espresso	912.233.5348	234 Bull Street	galleryespresso.com
Georgia Historical Society	912.651.2125	501 Whitaker Street	georgiahistory.com
Heavenly Spa by Westin	912.201.2000	1 Resort Drive	heavenlyspasavannah.com
Historic Savannah Foundation	912.233.7787	321 E. York Street	myhsf.org
Jazz'd Tapas Bar	912.236.7777	52 Barnard Street	jazzdsavannah.com
Jepson Center for the Arts	**912.790.8800**	**207 W. York Street**	**telfair.org**
Jim Pennington Fine Art	**985.789.5547**	**307 W. St. Julian Street**	**savannahcitymarket.com**
Juliette Gordon Low Birthplace	**912.233.4502**	**10 E. Oglethorpe Avenue**	**juliettegordonlowbirthplace.org**
Magnolia Spa	**912.373.2039**	**100 General McIntosh Boulevard**	**csspagroup.com**
Mighty Eighth Air Force Museum	912.748.8888	175 Bourne Avenue *(Pooler)*	mightyeighth.org
Moon River Brewing Company	**912.447.0943**	**21 W. Bay Street**	**moonriverbrewing.com**
Oatland Island	912. 395.1212	711 Sandtown Road	oatlandisland.org
Old Fort Jackson	**912.232.3945**	**1 Fort Jackson Road**	**chsgeorgia.org**

Poseidon Spa	912.721.5004	700 Drayton Street	mansiononforsythpark.com/poseidonspa
Raffine Galerie	**912.232.6400**	**306 W. Congress Street**	**raffinegalerie.com**
Red Gallery	912.525.4735	201 E. Broughton Street	
River Street Market Place	912.220.9101	502 E. River Street	riverstreetmarketplace.com
Romantic Weddings of Savannah	912.856.2165		romanticweddingsofsavannah.com
Roundhouse Railroad Museum	**912.651.6823**	**601 W. Harris Street**	**chsgeorgia.org**
Savannah Book Festival	912.897.9600	64 Palmer Boulevard	savannahbookfestival.org
Savannah Day Spa	912.234.9100	18 E. Oglethorpe Avenue	savannahdayspa.com
Savannah History Museum	**912.651.6840**	**303 MLK Jr. Boulevard**	**chsgeorgia.org**
Savannah Music Festival	**912.234.FEST**	**204 E. St. Julian Street, Suite 601**	**savannahmusicfestival.org**
Savannah Riverfront	**912.234.0295**	**404 E. Bay Street**	**riverstreetsavannah.com**
Savannah SandGnats	**912.351.9150**	**1401 E. Victory Drive**	**sandgnats.com**
Savannah Theatre Live Musical Shows	**912.233.7764**	**222 Bull Street**	**savannahtheatre.com**
SCAD Museum of Art	912.525.7191	227 MLK Jr. Boulevard	scad.edu/museum
Sentient Bean	912.232.4447	13 E. Park Avenue	sentientbean.com
Ships of the Sea Maritime Museum	912.232.1511	41 MLK Jr. Boulevard	shipsofthesea.org
Signature Gallery	**912.233.3082**	**303 W. St. Julian Street**	**signaturegallerysavannah.com**
Stephen Kasun Gallery	**407.474.0411**	**305-A W. Bryan Street**	**kasunstudio.com**
Sweet Water Spa	912.233.3288	148 Abercorn Street	termeacquadolce.com
Telfair Academy	**912.790.8800**	**121 Barnard Street**	**telfair.org**
Thomas Kinkade Gallery	**912.447.4660**	**211 W. St. Julian Street**	**thomaskinkadegallery.com**
Tybee Island Marine Science Center	**912.272.5008**	**1510 Strand Street**	**tybeemarinescience.org**
Tybee Tourism Council	**800.868.2322**		**tybeevisit.com**
Tybee Wedding Chapel	**888.988.9233**	**1112 US Highway 80**	**tybeeweddingchapel.com**
Wild Wing Café	**912.790.9464**	**27 Barnard St.**	**wildwingcafe.com**

Savannah Technical College | *p. 11, 79*

Savannah Music Festival | *p. 72*

Savannah Theatre | *p. 72*

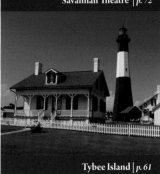

Tybee Island | *p. 61*

❖ DIRECTORY OF ADVERTISERS ❖

©Kevin Nightingale

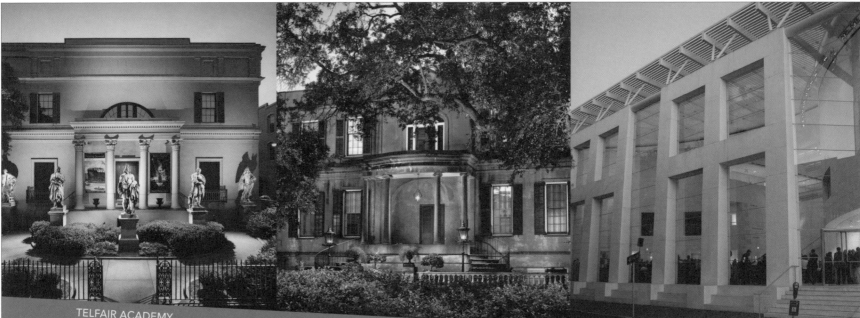